How to Use Psychological Leverage to Double the Power of What You Say

How to Use Psychological Leverage to Double the Power of What You Say

Les Donaldson

Parker Publishing Company, Inc.   West Nyack, New York

Library of Congress Cataloging in Publication Data

Donaldson, Les
   How to use psychological leverage to double the
power of what you say.

   1. Persuasion (Psychology) 2. Interpersonal
communication. I. Title.
BF637.P4D66   158'.2   77-12503
ISBN 0-13-437038-4

Printed in the United States of America

To my sons—
John, Dave and Jim

A PERSONAL NOTE FROM THE AUTHOR

The basic idea for Psychological Leverage evolved from my study of the writings and teachings presented by Psychological Associates of St. Louis, MO, in their Dimensional Management Training and Dimensional Sales and Sales Management instructor training programs. The philosophy of Psychological Associate's Dimensional Training Programs as expressed in *Dimensional Management Strategies* and *Effective Selling Through Psychology: Dimensional Sales and Sales Management Strategies* had a major impact upon my thinking in developing this book.

The flavor and philosophy of Psychological Leverage resulted from the ideas of client-centered therapy developed by Dr. Carl Rogers and from the booklet *Active Listening*, by Dr. Carl Rogers and Richard E. Farson.

The application of psychological techniques to practical everyday problems as described in this book are the result of a blending and testing of ideas in workshops and on-the-job application by myself and by many other people.

Les Donaldson

What This Book Will Do for You

This book will give you a psychological advantage in every interaction you have with people. It takes the myth out of psychology by explaining in everyday terms, and with specific everyday examples, how to apply "Psychological Leverage" when expressing your point of view. You'll learn simple techniques, developed by psychologists and tested in the field, that will multiply the effectiveness of what you say. You'll learn how to use Psychological Leverage to strengthen your influence on everyone. No matter how effective you are in dealing with people, this book will show you how to double your power to get things done.

For example, you'll learn how to use Psychological Leverage to gain cooperation from anyone, at any time, whenever needed. Once you understand the practical side of psychology, what makes people tick and how their personality determines their reactions, you will become more effective in your efforts to get people to listen. A system for getting others to listen, understand and cooperate, developed from the psychology of acceptance, awareness, "cognitive consistency," reinforcement, self-image and unfinished situations, has been tested in both business and social situations. If you apply this system and use these techniques in your dealings with people, you will be able to multiply the effectiveness of your words. You will develop the Psychological Leverage to overcome the obstacles that people place in your way.

You will learn to recognize and deal with the obstacles that keep people from accepting rules, your ideas and your opinions. You'll learn to overcome the mental and emotional obstacles that develop, for example, between parents and children or between managers and subordinates. You'll learn to use Psychological Leverage to overcome the barriers that keep people from listening to you.

You can use the same techniques in gaining understanding and acceptance from your peers and from your boss. You will be able to avoid conflict when presenting your ideas and opinions to people who normally disagree with you. You will be able to use psychological principles to explain your ideas and opinions in such a way that the people you deal with will listen and respond in a positive fashion.

You will also be able to overcome suspicion and resentment. You will develop more effective relationships with people because the techniques developed in this book eliminate the need for argument. They form a base for problem solving that will win respect and power.

Soon after you begin to use the techniques found in this book, you will find that your subordinates react in a more positive way. They will begin to make fewer and fewer excuses and try to learn better skills or systems to accomplish their assigned tasks. They will understand your goals and be more committed to them.

In the first three chapters of this book, you'll learn how to penetrate the barriers that keep people from listening. You'll also learn to recognize these barriers and understand their psychological causes. This understanding provides the base from which you will begin to develop Psychological Leverage.

Psychologists tell us that people only listen to things they have an interest in. They may start listening, but unless something is said that catches their interest, they will very quickly "tune out." The same is true of an audience listening to a speaker or one person listening to another.

People also tune out when something more pressing is on their mind. If they have some problem to solve or some project to complete, they tune out. Very often there is some preoccupation or emotional problem just below the surface in the other person's mind. These preoccupations may come to the surface at any time and cause the other person to stop listening to you.

Chapter Two explains how to utilize Psychological Leverage to penetrate these preoccupations, handle emotional outbreaks and capture the minds of other people. Psychologists have found that many of the techniques developed to counsel patients are effective in dealing with these preoccupations and emotional distractions in everyday affairs. Certain of these psychological principles that have been proven effective in counselling sessions, business meetings and social interactions are presented in this chapter. You can use these psychological principles when dealing with subordinates, family or friends, to release pent-up feelings, penetrate secretiveness, relieve emotional disturbances and clear out the obstacles that ordinarily interfere with attentive listening.

Chapter Three covers the strategy of "Psychological Timing." You can use the leverage of Psychological Timing to express your point of view when the chance for success is highest. You can overcome the obstacle of poor timing, and you'll be able to use Psychological Leverage to change poor timing into good timing. You can actually develop the specific conditions that are necessary for you to get your point of view across.

By using the simple psychological techniques explored in Chapter Four you will be able to gain more control in your dealings with other people. You will learn control techniques that you can use to enforce your decisions without aggressiveness, threat or coercion. You will learn to state your point of view in a way that will pay off for you in many ways.

In Chapter Five, you'll see how a new technique gives you Psychological Leverage when dealing with conflict. Often conflict is present in disguised form. You'll learn to recognize it, and diffuse it without becoming embroiled in bitter arguments.

Often people are argumentative and defensive about the way they are currently doing their job. They resist change. They persist in doing things the old way in spite of clear orders to the contrary, and they try to bulldoze others into accepting their way. They become stubborn and egotistical and fight over inconsequential differences. Often they become emotional and angry. You can develop Psychological Leverage to deal with and neutralize these problems.

Additional techniques have been developed to help get your ideas across clearly and concisely. A clear and concise message is more easily understood. Techniques to help improve understanding are presented in Chapter Six.

Idea acceptance is related to internal motivation. Behavioral scientists have established a number of principles which can be used in everyday affairs to relate an idea to the motivation of the other person. By relating your ideas to those motivations, you have the best chance of getting your idea accepted.

These concepts, principles and techniques are presented in everyday terms and are applied, in Chapter Six, to the problems of gaining understanding and acceptance of ideas.

In Chapter Seven you'll learn how to use the "Linking Technique" to gain this acceptance and motivate people to higher levels of performance.

A large amount of scientific research has shown that people who clearly see the relationship between their work and the work of the organization as a whole become more productive. The reason for the increase is related to the person's commitment. Chapter Eight provides you with techniques that can be used to develop this commitment.

Productivity is also related to the trust and confidence that people have in you. In Chapter Nine, you'll see how to use Psychological Leverage to win people's minds and in Chapter Ten you'll learn the techniques of winning trust and confidence.

Chapters Eleven and Twelve show you how to develop a winning reputation and double the power of what you say. Chapter Eleven outlines methods for warding off criticism and gives you techniques for handling it when it does occur. Chapter Twelve shows how to develop a strong power base and explains speech techniques that denote power.

Chapter Thirteen covers group meetings of all kinds and shows how to make them more productive. You can be sure of getting good results from every group meeting you conduct by using the Psychological Leverage developed from the concepts in this book.

You will learn to mentally predict what people are likely to say in various situations. By learning the techniques covered in Chapter Fourteen, you will be able to come fairly close with these predictions. By analyzing the motivation of people in relation to certain situations, you will be able to determine ahead of time the approach each person will take. This will give you the advantage of preparing in advance what you wish to say, so that you will have maximum impact.

If you are a member of an organization and are trying to get a promotion, Chapter Fifteen offers some guidelines that will help you. The results you get from using the other techniques in this book will place you in a strong personal position.

The techniques developed in this book have been tested by the author. They may be used to improve relationships with people in any and all situations. You can use them in dealing with business associates, friends, tradesmen, family or neighbors—anyone. You will gain better understanding, trust and respect from all these people if you practice these methods daily. If you do practice, the use of these psychology-based techniques will surely double the power of what you say.

Les Donaldson

Table of Contents

How to Use Psychological Leverage
to Double the Power of What You Say

1 ━━━━━

How to Use Psychological Leverage to Break Down Listening Barriers

You can very rapidly develop the "Psychological Leverage" needed to overcome listening barriers. You can do this by practicing, one by one, the simple psychology-based techniques developed in this book.

People often erect listening barriers that block out most of what you say. By learning to recognize listening barriers and by understanding their causes, you can effectively neutralize them. You will gain Psychological Leverage by understanding the psychological cause for these emotions, habits and preoccupations. Professional techniques, developed by psychologists, provide the leverage that will penetrate these barriers. You can use them to become a powerful influence in your daily interactions with people.

PSYCHOLOGICAL BARRIERS THAT KEEP PEOPLE FROM LISTENING

One of the most common reasons for the trouble you have in getting your point of view understood is the tendency of people to be inattentive. They are unable to be attentive and listen carefully because they are continually drawn to more pressing thoughts. Often these thoughts are so psychologically compelling that people can't resist them and your message is blocked out. Trying to talk to someone who is drawn to more pressing thoughts is like talking to someone who has a clear plastic soundproof helmet over his head. You can see through the helmet but your words are blocked out. You are unable to penetrate his consciousness.

Often these barriers are erected due to unconscious causes. These hidden forces interfere and block out your message without any awareness by the other person that he is resisting. There are tip-offs you can recognize that will enable you to penetrate these unconscious barriers to listening.

People also *consciously* erect barriers to understanding. A person may be so anxious to speak himself that he will block out your message while attempting to force through his own. Psychologists have identified a number of these barriers that block understanding. I have arranged them in three broad categories for easier examination. They are emotional distractions, habitual distractions and preoccupations with "unfinished" activities.

SIX EMOTIONAL DISTRACTIONS THAT REQUIRE RECOGNITION

All six of the emotionally generated distractions interfere with listening. Each of the six distractions that follow diverts the mind away from discussion toward the distraction:

1. Anger due to frustration.
2. Anxiety over the unknown.
3. Fear of the loss of security.
4. Excitement over happiness.
5. Tension due to deprived needs.
6. Boredom.

The primary activity of our brain is directed by imagery or picture formation. If the picture is clear and serene, we are able to flit from thought to thought or listen to those things that we find interesting. As soon as some form of danger, deprivation, joy, or any frustrating incident occurs, an image forms and prepares us for action. A tension or excitation develops across the nervous system and our mental energy is concentrated on a search for the appropriate method to deal with the tension-related problem.

The expression of emotional feelings of tension requires mental activity. This mental activity interferes with listening. When we are emotionally upset, the primary energy of our brain is directed toward the dissipation of the emotional tension. It becomes a barrier that interferes with listening and understanding.

This mental activity intensifies in relation to the importance of the threat or problem. In the case of immediate danger, full attention is concentrated on the danger. You would not expect someone facing immediate danger to divert his attention from that danger and listen to an idea you might wish to express.

In our daily discussions we seldom encounter cases of extreme danger, but we do encounter frustrating situations. As a matter of fact, psychologists have found that even minor emotional tension directs our mental activity to the source of the tension and away from attention to other things, such as the conversation at hand.

Emotional tension, even in mild form, interferes with listening. It becomes a barrier that keeps you from getting your message across. Your success in dealing with tense people will be determined more by *how* you say it than by *what* you say. When you recognize tension in someone you are talking to, you must deal with the tension before dealing with your own message.

How an Emotional Distraction Interfered with a Job Assignment. The manager of a midwestern manufacturing plant recently told me about a problem he had experienced with one of his foremen. The foreman was so preoccupied with more compelling thoughts that he actually did not hear what the manager said to him in a face-to-face conversation. Jim, the plant manager, walked up to Bill, the foreman, and explained a new system he wanted to install that would increase productivity. The new system, developed by their engineers, would increase productivity by ten percent. Jim explained that most of the machinery would have to be rearranged to make room for a new assembly platform.

Bill kept glancing away and appeared to be very inattentive. Jim thought Bill seemed quite tense. He was nervous and was not concentrating on what was being said. At one point Bill actually started to walk away. Jim stopped him. "Can you start rearranging the machinery Monday?" Jim asked. Bill turned around and said, "Why do you want the machinery moved?" Obviously, Bill had not heard Jim's previous explanation. A barrier to listening had been erected that blocked out Jim's message.

Jim could have criticized Bill for not listening. He might have become angry or sarcastic or asked Bill why he didn't pay attention. These things would only have worsened the situation. Bill might then have become angry himself and the chances for understanding would have been further reduced. Fortunately, Jim recognized Bill's tense actions and refrained from any hostility.

Jim talked to Bill about his tension rather than pressing the discussion about the new system. He asked what had happened to cause Bill's nervousness. Bill said he had just been involved in a confrontation with two operators over their work load. The two operators had started a slow-down. If they continued the slow-down, production would be out of balance, creating a problem for the next shift. By concentrating on Bill's emotional distraction, Jim gave Bill the opportunity to express the concerns he felt about production.

Bill's entire attention was directed to the slow-down. He still had the confrontation in mind. He knew repairs had to be made on the machinery the two men were working with, but could not get the repairs made until the end of the shift. Bill's attention was directed to those two machines. He was making sure that he would see any problem that developed with the two machines, in order to make immediate corrections. Jim waited until Bill's problem was corrected at the end of the shift, and then resumed discussing the installation of the new assembly platform.

If Jim had become irritated and had directed anger or criticism at Bill during a time of emotional disturbance, he would most likely have evoked anger and a hostile reply from Bill. Psychologists tell us people who are emotionally upset are more easily frustrated and will spontaneously react in anger.

Resorting to anger in a frustrating situation is a normal out-growth of our biological motivation for self-preservation. Cavemen, for example, who became frustrated in life or death situations would become angry. In anger they would yell and make harsh sounds in an effort to scare away danger. In these anger-provoking situations a fear-related tenseness develops across the nervous system. This tenseness directs the full attention of the brain to the danger at hand. Today we still experience emotional tension in reaction to frustrating situations. This tension directs our mental activity and may become a barrier to listening.

1. HOW TO DEAL WITH ANGER

The first of the six emotional distractions is anger. Anger grows out of the frustration that occurs when some form of interference blocks the accomplishment of a goal. This blocking may occur as the result of even the slightest criticism if it coincides with the person's attempts to reach some goal. The resulting anger will be directed at the frustration and will block out anything being said.

Any attempt at conversation or persuasion will be wasted at this point. The person you are talking to will not hear a word that is said. Argument will only add fuel to the fire. Since he is gearing up for an attack upon the frustrating element, you may become the object of the attack, whether or not you deserve it. You can successfully make your point only after his anger has subsided. *You can improve, even* double, your chances of being understood if you give an angry person time to expend his anger, before expressing your point of view.

You can help the other person expend his anger and put him in a more reasonable state of mind by:

1. Telling him that you understand his anger.
2. Showing your interest by asking for the cause of the anger.
3. Allowing the angry person time, by remaining silent yourself, to verbally expend his anger.

Once the anger is expended, he will become less resistive to what you have to tell him. Your message will get through.

2. HOW TO DEAL WITH ANXIETY

Anxiety, the second emotional distraction, produces emotional tension. Most people fear the unknown. When a person approaches a strange or unknown situation, he may feel somewhat anxious. You may expect inattention from anxious people, just as you do from angry people. Again, they are mentally working to prepare for some unknown danger.

If you call a subordinate into your office, he may feel anxious simply because he doesn't know what to expect. He may wonder if you are going to criticize him or restrict his power or limit his freedom in some way. To reduce anxiety, state your reason for meeting early in the conversation. Unless there is no doubt about the reason for the meeting, this anxiety may develop and interfere with the subordinate's listening. After the initial greeting you should immediately state the reason. If Jim, in our earlier example, had called Bill into his office he would have said, "Bill, I've called you in to talk about installing a new assembly system."

3. HOW TO DEAL WITH INSECURITY

Deep-seated fear of the loss of security, the third distraction, may also produce an emotional reaction. Some people may be so insecure in their job or so low in self-confidence that they continually await the "falling of the ax." Just being notified that you wish to talk to them may cause them to feel their job is in jeopardy. Their fears are so deep-seated that they become suspicious and expect even praise to be followed by some serious reprimand or even discharge.

Most of the time their fear directs their mental activity, their thoughts, away from listening. They frequently misinterpret messages by forming mental images that are based more upon their fears than upon the actual words used. You can determine whether or not you are getting through to this type of person by asking frequent questions. *You may determine their understanding by asking for their comments or summaries of what you said.*

In the discussion of the new assembly platform, Jim might have asked Bill for his comments. He might have asked, "Bill, *what do you think* will be the easiest way to move the machinery?" Or, "What day would be best, *in your opinion*, to make the change?" After the plan for installing the new platform was explained, he might have asked, "Bill, would you summarize the steps in installing the platform, *as you see them.*"

4. HOW TO DEAL WITH EXCITEMENT

The excitement of happiness, success or love is also an emotional distraction. The joy of a new job, baby, home or car may instill such excitement that all else is blocked out. This person is simply not going to listen to you. You would do well to take a few minutes and participate in his excitement. Any attempt to persuade will be fruitless at this time. *Always give the excited person an opportunity to express his emotional feelings before trying to express your point of view.*

5. HOW TO DEAL WITH TENSION

Tension, the fifth distraction, occurs as a result of being deprived of some need. This tension again directs our mental activity toward the distraction. If we have been deprived of sleep, food, water or good health, our mental activity is directed toward these deprivations and away from conversation. If we have lost a job, money, love or security, our attention will only be attracted to statements that have relevance to our loss.

We all have social needs and they are more important to us as we become deprived of them. If we are denied the opportunity to chat with friends, we feel deprived and concentrate our energies on finding opportunities to satisfy this need. If a subordinate seems inclined to jump from topic to topic during your conversation, he may be trying to lengthen the conversation to fulfill his social need.

People who continually try to tell you what to do or how to do it;

who explain the great results they are always getting; who take stubborn positions; who argue and monopolize the conversation; who try to force, intimidate or manipulate you, may be seeking recognition. They may feel deprived of recognition for their accomplishments or may simply have formed those habits as a method of seeking recognition. In any event, they are not listening or trying to understand your point of view. *All of the emotion-related tensions must be allowed to subside before you can make your point. This is how you relate to the psychology of the other person.*

6. HOW TO DEAL WITH BOREDOM

Perhaps the final emotional obstacle to listening, boredom, should be called a neutral emotion. It's more an absence of an emotion. Boredom is a mental state that results from a lack of interesting stimuli. If what you say is not related to some need or area of interest of the other person, his mind may wander to other more interesting things. *You must create pictures with what you say, that arouse his interest and relate to his needs, if you wish to hold his attention.*

FIVE HABITS THAT BLOCK UNDERSTANDING

Defensiveness, aggressiveness, superficial agreement, suspiciousness and inattention are habits that block understanding. Habits are two-edged swords. They simplify our existence by making possible such instantaneous activities as ducking or dodging danger, walking, talking and work skills. At the same time they interfere with our attempts to change when we face different situations or changing conditions. They impede our progress when we are trying to learn new responses or new variations in the movements required to perform new skills.

Habits often persist long after the conditions that required their development have disappeared. They then become barriers that hinder our results. I have a friend, for example, who had problems with people for years because he was habitually sarcastic when talking. When made aware that he had hurt someone's feelings, he was truly sorry and often indicated that he was going to stop making sarcastic remarks. In spite of his desire to stop using sarcastic remarks, they seemed to just slip out.

In an attempt to determine how he had developed such a deep-seated habit, I listened closely, over a period of years, and analyzed the situations that produced the sarcasm. At first there seemed to be no pattern. He was sarcastic to people from all walks of life. He spread sarcasm over a wide range of topics and he was equally sarcastic whether tired, refreshed, ill or in good health. Finally, a chance remark led me to the answer. He dropped one of his most intellectually sarcastic statements, and then said: "That one was worthy of Will Bender." Upon questioning, I discovered Will Bender was one of a group of intellectual verbal combatants with whom my friend had associated in college. Each member of the group was expected to develop and use intellectual barbs to retain membership in the group. My friend had developed a natural "caustic tongue" as a method of protecting his image in the group.

The pattern I had not seen before was now quite clear. My friend became sarcastic in any intellectually stimulating situation. He was automatically reverting to a previously established method of demonstrating his intelligence. Once my friend became fully aware of how this habit had developed and how his behavior was being controlled by unconscious ties to past situations, he was able to start extinguishing the habit. *You can penetrate the unconscious psychological drives of the people you deal with by asking questions designed to uncover the causes of their non-productive habits.*

Often people develop habitual behavior patterns as defense mechanisms. They cover intellectual weaknesses by bluffing or by pretending that only their own position is reasonable. They habitually proclaim their greatness—what they have done, how much they have made, how great their achievements are—to fulfill their status needs. Long after the needs are fulfilled or the reasons for these habits have disappeared, the habit persists. Habits of this type become barriers in conversation and impede listening.

1. DEFENSIVENESS—HOW TO DEAL WITH IT

There are five habitual distractions that interfere with understanding. One of the most difficult of these barriers to overcome is habitual defensiveness. Some people develop a pattern of defensiveness that pervades every aspect of their lives. If you ask one of these people what his results for the day are, he will begin defending his results before he gives you the figures.

This person may have developed the habit in some overly critical atmosphere where he was constantly challenged about the quality or quantity of his work. Now that he is out of that critical environment and no longer needs to be defensive, his defensive reactions are the result of habit. Current circumstances that are similar to the old situation trigger this defensiveness.

Defensiveness interferes with listening and blocks out the possibility of learning. It is counter productive. Defensiveness is an outward-directed mental activity aimed at eliminating a real or imagined threat. Since all this person's activity is concentrated on defensiveness, he will be unable to listen. You will need to overcome this habitual defensive action before he will listen and understand what you say. *You can use Psychological Leverage here. Let him defend his position, assure him you understand, and then present your views.*

You can use the following four-point guideline in dealing with defensiveness:

1. Give the defensive person some confidential information. You may share some secret or tell him some error that you have made. This will help gain his trust.
2. Listen carefully to his defensive statements. This will show that you are sincerely interested.
3. Assure him that you understand his defensiveness. Tell him that his reasons seem to support his reactions.
4. Present your own view after you have shown him that you are interested in and understand him.

2. DEALING WITH HABITUAL AGGRESSIVENESS

Habitual aggressiveness is developed in the same way as defensiveness. People become aggressive in a competitive environment and often this aggressiveness becomes habitual. Then it is carried over into other situations. The aggressive person does not usually realize that his aggressive habit is interfering with his mental receptivity and that he is closing his mind to incoming messages.

In conversation, aggressive people become argumentative. They become defensive and resist change. When you initiate new policies, you'll find them clinging to the old. These stubborn reactions are habitual and are difficult to overcome. They can be overcome, however, if you are patient and resist the temptation to argue or force your point across. *You can gain Psychological Leverage by letting them expend their anger through conversation.*

3. HOW TO DETECT SUPERFICIAL AGREEMENT

Superficial agreement is often more deceptive than habitual defensiveness or aggressiveness. The person who agrees with you without thought or consideration is not really accepting your point of view. He is simply avoiding the issue. Many people will pretend to agree in order to avoid arguing. They feel that an unpleasant situation will arise if they make their disagreement known. In order to avoid what to them would be an unpleasant situation, they pretend to agree. Habitual agreement becomes a defense against presenting what might be an unpopular position.

The agreeable subordinate doesn't confront situations that he believes will result in disapproval. Neither will he question directions from you that may cause problems in the work gang. He pretends agreement, knowing he will not carry out your instructions. When questioned later, he will develop all sorts of excuses to explain why he did not follow your instructions. *You can double your power in this situation by using direct questions to penetrate his superficial answers and eliminate the possibility of later excuses.*

4. HABITUAL SUSPICIOUSNESS

The habitually suspicious person is usually secretive. Because of an earlier experience in which he was manipulated, tricked or cheated, he has developed this habitual suspiciousness in order to avoid being taken advantage of. The secretiveness becomes a habit and the habit interferes with understanding in conversation. Thorough questioning is required to determine the opinions of secretive or habitually suspicious people.

5. HABITUAL INATTENTION

Habitual inattention can result from the previously discussed distractions or from a lack of interest. Inattention develops due to lack of interest in the subject or a lack of interest in the person speaking. After attending a number of functions that are uninteresting, a person may come to expect all similar functions to be uninteresting. Inattention soon becomes a habit in all similar situations.

Inattention may also occur simply as a result of being bored. The material being presented may not be stated in a clear and understandable way. Or the topic matter may simply not be interesting to some people. Inattention also results from the message content. *Inattention is recognizable and may be altered by relating your remarks in some way to known areas of interest of the inattentive person.*

HOW "UNFINISHED ACTIONS" BLOCK UNDERSTANDING

Suppose a sales subordinate comes into your office obviously excited, and starts to tell you about the big sale he just concluded. Suppose at this point you ask him to hold off and help you finish your next month's projections before completing his story. He will, in all probability, make a number of mistakes. By blocking his emotional drive to relate his success story, you force a suppression of his natural action and create an "unfinished action."

Inner-directed attention results when some inner thought is more compelling than the immediate discussion. This inner-directing of attention is usually directed at an unfinished action.

To understand the importance of completing an unfinished action, a brief explanation from *Gestalt* psychology would be helpful. The German word *Gestalt* has been defined by Perls (1951), as follows: "Configuration, structure, theme, structural relationship (Korzybski) or meaningful organized whole most closely approximate the originally German word *Gestalt*. . . . (p. ix)." To simplify the definition for the purpose of this discussion, the word "pattern" will be used.

To illustrate this point, we can take a plain piece of paper and draw a series of dots or dashes across the center of the page. Our mind will complete the pattern. We will perceive the paper as having been separated into two sections. We tend to see the paper as now being divided into two "whole" sections, rather than the one "whole" it was before. This is a result of our mind registering the series of dots as a separating line, in order to complete the pattern.

Our human need for a logical, rational, organized world has been proposed as the explanation for this process of mentally completing a pattern or an action. If something happens that prevents us from forming the *gestalt* or leaves us with an unfinished action, we have an unhealthy psychological condition. We become frustrated and anxious and this interferes with our listening and our understanding.

In synthesizing the information on *gestalt* formation, unfinished situation, human needs for expression, and Freud's discussion of repression and the resulting interference with normal functioning (p. 12), we can explain the psychological cause of inattention. We can explain why people don't listen. That reason, very simply, is that they can't. Their attention is turned inwardly to the unfinished action. Inattention or lack of listening will occur whenever one of these unfinished actions is more pressing than the topic being discussed.

The Three Forms of Unfinished Actions

The unfinished fulfillment of human needs, interrupted thoughts, speech or activities, and the blocking of emotional expression are the three forms of unfinished activities that interfere with listening and understanding.

We fulfill many of our human needs through conversation. Just as we fulfill our social needs through conversation, we also fulfill our esteem and other ego-related needs in the same way. If we imagine that others do not recognize our abilities or knowledge or our accomplishments, we seek this recognition through conversation. We hint, tell outright, or brag about what we know, can do or have done.

We fulfill many of our biological, security, social, independence and self-realization needs in this way. We barter in the fulfillment of our biological and security needs; we chat about sports, social or business interests in the fulfillment of our social needs; we try to persuade others in the fulfillment of our independence needs; and we practice speech techniques, to learn from others, to fulfill our self-realization needs. All of our needs can be fulfilled through conversation and the blocking of this conversation can create an unfinished activity, which becomes a barrier to listening.

If a subordinate is trying to give you a lot of details about a particular market, there may be more involved than just a market report. He may be trying to gain recognition for the fine job he did in researching the market. He may also be using the report as an instrument to point out his wide variety of talents. This may be completely unconscious on his part.

The desire to fulfill ego-related needs is often unconscious. The most blatant, outspoken individual may not be aware that he is attempting to fulfill his esteem needs through conversation. If the conversation does not follow a pattern that permits the completion of this ego-directed search for esteem, we have an unfinished activity —an unfinished fulfillment of human needs—that may result in inattention.

Interrupted thoughts, speech or activities all have the same consequence—inattention. The salesman who walks in on a buyer who is in the midst of a business activity, and interrupts that buyer, is blocking the buyer's internal drive for completion. The same is true if he interrupts the buyer's speech or thoughts. The natural functioning of the organism is impeded. This interference leads to inattention.

Suppressed emotional reactions are the most troublesome of the three forms of unfinished activities. They immediately interfere with listening and understanding. The more they are suppressed the more they intensify. Mild irritation can build into anger and irrational behavior very quickly. If these emotions are not allowed to ventilate through conversation, they completely block out the possibility of attention or understanding.

Creating a Psychological Obligation for the Other Person to Listen

Once you have removed these three major categories of listening barriers—emotions, habits and preoccupations—you can be twice as effective with what you say. The person you talk to will hear twice as much, will understand twice as much, and will remember twice as much.

The way to accomplish the task of overcoming these barriers is to encourage the other person to clear his mind through conversation. You do this by listening without criticism and by asking questions for clarification. This process builds the Psychological Leverage that you may need to make your point. *The fact that you listened without criticism creates a psychological obligation on the other person to listen to you.*

A FOUR-STEP PLAN TO DETERMINE PEOPLE'S WILLINGNESS TO LISTEN

Checking for Feelings of Fear or Suspicion

Many subordinates feel suspicious or fearful when called in or approached by a superior. They preoccupy themselves with these fears and suspicions and consequently do not listen carefully. They have their minds and ears pre-set to pick up harsh and unjust criticism. They are not tuned in for the constructive message you are trying to get across.

One way to test the other person's feelings is to state the purpose of your meeting or business in very clear and concise terms. When the purpose is stated in such a manner many of the other's fears will disappear. Before you continue, give him an opportunity to respond to the purpose you stated. His response will reveal his feelings. If he is fearful or suspicious his remarks will show it.

If he comments on your purpose or asks some question relating to the purpose, he is willing to listen. Should his answer concern some problem or be irrelevant to the purpose, he is not ready to listen.

Sometimes a subordinate will give verbal indications of attention when he is not really interested. One way to check this is to *watch for non-verbal clues.* If the subordinate is fidgeting around, tapping his finger, bouncing his knees, or shuffling his feet, he is indicating some preoccupation. Something is interfering with his normal functioning. If he starts "doodling" or writing or reading, this is a clear indication that his mental activity is not concentrated on your topic.

Smugness, extreme silence, or looking or walking away are also clues of inattention. The smug subordinate may be indicating, "I'll do as I darn well please." Extreme silence may indicate suspicion or distrust and a reluctance to discuss a topic that might create problems or unpleasantness.

These non-verbal as well as verbal clues must be assessed and dealt with. The underlying situation must be explored and listened to so the subordinate can complete the unfinished activity and you can complete the task at hand.

Using an "Interest Facilitator"

You may check the other person's level of interest by using an "Interest Facilitator." Relate your initial remarks to one of his known areas of interest. If he immediately interrupts you or changes the subject, you must deal with the interruption or the new subject before you can gain his attention.

Someone who changes the subject is obviously telling you your topic did not interest him. If he continually changes the subject, that may be an indication that he has some fear of discussing your original topic. That subject must then be confronted. You must find out what reservations the other person has before you can get him to open his mind to your evidence.

Interrupting, an indication of non-listening, is sometimes a sign of interest. It is interest from his own point of view, however, and it is interest in getting you to accept his point of view without his having to evaluate yours. Regardless of the other's intent, interrupting should be viewed as an indication of inattentiveness.

Testing with the "Benefit Projection" Technique

You should project a benefit that you believe will interest the person to whom you are speaking. Projecting a benefit helps him visualize how his personal involvement may lead to receiving the benefit. If the benefit does not appeal to him, he will probably say so and you may try projecting a new benefit. If the benefit is appealing, he will indicate his interest in your topic. If he has some reservations, he may, induced by the mentioned benefit, bring those reservations out in the open.

You may also speculate as to the cause of some problem. Again, if your speculation is wrong, the other person will nearly always set you straight. Even the most tight-lipped people, who usually won't give you any information, will at least let you know that you are wrong. You can use this psychological technique, stating an incorrect assumption, to develop interest and draw the other person into the conversation. This technique also penetrates secretiveness.

If you mention the possibility that there is a problem or relate a new idea to the topic, the other person will usually respond. He may discuss how the new idea will work, or what effects the new idea might have. He might discuss ways of solving the problem. He may also introduce additional problems. Any of these actions indicate an active level of interest.

Using a Functional Questioning Technique

Any successful salesman will tell you that selling is impossible without asking questions. This holds true for any form of persuasion. In order to get your point across, you must understand the mood, objections and receptivity of the other person. Unless he tells you these things himself, they are difficult to determine.

So, you ask questions to determine the other's willingness to listen. A question can be tied in very nicely to the statements of purpose or it can be tied into the benefit. If you are trying to get a subordinate to work nights, you might proceed as follows: "Joe, I would like to talk to you about switching to the night shift [purpose]. I believe the extra experience will help you get the next foreman promotion that comes up [benefit]. How would you feel about going on nights [question related to purpose]?

In this example, the question is related to the purpose of the meeting. That will test the subordinate's interest in working nights. You could relate the question to the benefit. You might ask: "How do you feel about working toward a promotion?" The answer will determine the direction for the balance of the discussion.

The most powerful method of developing a subordinate's interest in a topic is to ask him for his feelings, ideas, opinions and recommendations. When you ask for his feelings, if he is not interested he will make his lack of interest known. As he gives his ideas, opinions and recommendations, his areas of interest will evolve. The areas in which he lacks interest will also evolve and those can be noted as areas of inattention.

Occasionally you will encounter a subordinate who is so suspicious and secretive that he will actually resist answering your questions. He will simply look away or stare at you and say nothing. You can resolve this problem simply by confronting this new situation with a new question. You might say: "Joe, you seem to be reluctant to answer my question. Is something wrong?" Stay with this line of questioning until you get a response.

How One Salesman Waited Out His Customer's "Unfinished Actions." A salesman once told me that one of his customers continually ignored his sales presentation. He said the customer stared out the window or looked at papers on his desk. The customer occasionally grunted or mumbled but never really paid attention to the salesman.

I advised the salesman to "wait out" the customer's distracting habits on his next call. When making his next call, the salesman stopped talking when the customer looked out the window. After what seemed an eternity to the salesman, the customer turned and told him to continue his presentation.

Thereafter, each time the customer looked out the window or started reading, the salesman stopped talking until the customer commented on his presentation. This salesman's willingness to let the customer complete his unfinished actions resulted in continually improving sales.

A CHECKLIST OF LISTENING BARRIERS

Preoccupation with distracting thoughts causes inattention. People reveal these distracting barriers by unconsciously giving both spoken and non-verbal clues. You can use the following checklist of clues to listening barriers to tell when people are inattentive. You can then do something to regain their attention. The clues are:

1. Interrupting your statements
2. Making sarcastic remarks
3. Making flat assertions
4. Giving superficial agreement
5. Avoiding taking a position
6. Making excuses
7. Any expression of emotion
8. Expressions of suspicion
9. Fidgeting
10. Tapping fingers
11. Bouncing knees
12. Shuffling feet
13. Twiddling fingers
14. Looking out window
15. Slips of the tongue
16. Irrelevant remarks
17. Reading or writing
18. Extended silence
19. Refusal to answer questions
20. Any nervous movement or non-related activity

2

How to Recognize and Deal With "Emotional Interference"

In Chapter One you saw how psychological barriers direct people's attention away from the conversation at hand and you saw how to overcome these barriers effectively. In this chapter you will learn to recognize, understand and eliminate emotional interference that blocks understanding. Tip-offs to emotional interference are identified and specific techniques for reducing the interference that have been tested in everyday situations are presented.

Emotional interference can be thought of as an unfinished activity. When a person is upset, he feels an emotional tension. This tension persists until the individual takes some action to complete his unfinished activity. As long as an individual is prevented from expressing the emotion that accompanies any frustration he encounters, he will turn his attention inwardly to the emotion—the unfinished activity.

THE FINE ART OF PASSIVE LISTENING

As a first step in your program of doubling the power of what you say, train yourself to listen without comment when someone you are talking to seems angry or upset. This is known as "passive listening." Passive listening will give you the leverage to get them to listen to you once their unfinished activity is complete. When you listen to others, they feel obligated to listen to you in return.

If you are aware that the person you are talking to is mentally distracted, you can eliminate the distraction by using the passive listening technique. Often, however, people disguise or suppress these distractions. You can determine when this has happened and avoid wasting your persuasive efforts by listening carefully to what people say. They will give tip-offs in their conversation that expose these distractions.

FIVE TIP-OFFS TO "EMOTIONAL INTERFERENCE"

Defensive actions that act as "mind guards," frustrations that trigger anger, excitement, non-verbal and irrational actions are tip-offs that an individual is preoccupied with other thoughts. All of these tip-offs should be recognized as indicators of "emotional interference," interference that blocks understanding.

I remember sitting in on a discussion of production cost estimates for a new contract between a production plant manager and his controller. The manager, after discussing the importance of the contract, asked the controller to work a few hours late that night to get the job done, prior to an 8 A.M. meeting the next day.

The controller became uneasy and made derogatory remarks about engineering and production. His tone of voice was very aggressive. The manager recognized that the controller was upset and asked the controller to let him know later in the day about working late. The controller's aggressiveness was a tip-off to an emotionally distracting frustration. There are five tip-offs of this type, although they are often more subtle, that tell you when the other person is emotionally distracted.

Recognizing "Mind Guards"

Blaming others by accusation or by derogatory remarks is a defensive action used as a "mind guard" against threat. Other defensive actions that are tip-offs to emotional interference are aggression, unreasonableness, stubbornness and sarcasm. A person displaying any of these tendencies feels he has been or is about to be criticized, degraded or endangered in some way. The fact that he may be completely mistaken does not alter his feelings. He is reacting to what he feels is a real threat.

We all develop defensive actions to ward off real threat. Often they become defenses against threats to our image of ourselves. If something threatens our image, we tend to become defensive to protect our self-image. If we picture ourselves as outstanding performers and are unable to get rewards commensurate with this performance, we may feel a threat. Our inability to get satisfactory rewards points out a discrepancy between our opinion and our boss' opinion. We must now face the possibility that we are mistaken about our own performance, or we must become defensive. It is much easier to blame the boss. Often we take the easy way out and blame him rather than reevaluate our own performance.

Understanding "Mental Triggers"

Pouting, scowling, subtle sarcasm, anger and explicit sarcasm are mentally triggered tip-offs to frustration-related emotional interference. Frustration occurs when we are unable to reach some goal or when some need is blocked. When the fulfillment of a need is interfered with, we feel tension. If the tension is strong enough it releases a "mental trigger" which produces aggression. When the accountant in the previous example was asked to work a few hours late, he became angry and aggressive. He became critical of engineering and said he had more important things to do. He was frustrated because working late would interfere with his previously made plans.

The controller expressed his frustration aggressively, but people often express frustration in a more subdued way. People express their frustration aggressively or submissively depending upon the situation. If they feel free to express anger or sarcasm, without punishment, they will do so. If they fear repercussions, they turn to pouting, scowling or subtle sarcasm.

Listening for Excitement

Often a person is so engrossed in his happiness that he fails to hear you at all. When he denies that he heard your instructions, he is not necessarily lying; he simply was too "turned on" to hear what you said. The excitement of happiness or joy is just as distracting as anger.

When you encounter excited or joyous persons, remember that they are distracted from your message until their joy or excitement is ventilated. *Overly enthusiastic remarks, trembling, rising voice levels and nonsensical remarks showing excitement are tip-offs to emotional interference.*

Testing Non-Verbal Actions

People often glance away or write or read while you are trying to talk to them. These actions are clues that the other person is mentally distracted. When the other person scowls, sighs, purses his lips, twitches or taps his fingers or makes similar nervous movements, he is giving non-verbal clues that he is mentally distracted.

Recognizing Irrational Actions

Ranting, raving, a reddened face, clenched fists or verbal threats of violence are irrational actions and are tip-offs to possible danger. When enraged, people may resort to irrational actions. This activity, an attempt to eliminate real or imagined impending danger, may result in harm to those close by. Stay at a safe distance while permitting an enraged person to ventilate his anger.

Usually an enraged person will work out his anger very rapidly. The high level of activity ventilates the anger more rapidly than usual. The best course of action is passive listening. Remain quiet and let him rant and rave until his anger subsides.

How Recognizing the Non-Verbal Indications of Violence Kept Three Men Out of Trouble. I was walking through a shopping center in St. Louis, Missouri, one evening with two friends, when a man slammed through two swinging doors into the walkway directly in front of us. The man was large enough to be a football player. He was approximately six feet tall and weighed about two hundred and eighty pounds.

Another man approaching from the opposite direction said "Hi" to the big man as he passed him by. The big man turned toward the passing man, who was now directly to our right. The big man's face was red, his fists were clenched, and his eyes were drawn into small beads.

As the big man turned toward us, his eyes looked like beads on a rifle and they were zeroed in on the passing stranger. I whispered to my friends not to say anything. Just then my suspicions were confirmed. The big man was in an irrational state. He blurted out, "I can kill him!" He was right in front of us now. We tried to move around him, but he blocked our way. We stopped momentarily. "I can break his neck," the big man continued. We still remained quiet. Passive listening was the only logical recourse. The passing stranger had put twenty or twenty five feet between himself and our group by then. The big man said, "I can punch his head off!" I now noticed that normal color had returned to his face and he relaxed his fists. We still remained quiet. He paused for a few minutes, looking at us, and then started walking away. Our passive listening permitted him to verbally expend his anger without striking anyone.

The stranger who had innocently said "Hi" to the big man triggered an irrational reaction because the big man was already enraged. In his enraged state he was not thinking clearly and saw the most innocent comment as a challenge or ridicule. If we had said anything at all while the big man was enraged, he might have turned his anger on us.

TWO TECHNIQUES THAT REDUCE EMOTIONAL INTERFERENCE

There are two important points to be remembered about emotional interference if you are to deal with people effectively. One, a person may be emotionally upset when you first encounter him. He may seem calm and receptive but may actually be angry or in a very anxious state of mind. Second, your behavior may cause the other person to intensify his emotional feelings which interfere with his ability to listen and understand what you say. You may, with your way of speaking, cause him to intensify an angry feeling and become more emotionally distracted. On the other hand, the way you speak can reduce the other's tension and anger.

The benefit from this principle is that you can lead the person who is emotionally upset into a more rational and receptive state. If you encounter a person who seems to be anxious, provoked, angry or preoccupied in any way, you can use questioning techniques, developed in this chapter, to help him ventilate his emotions. As the emotions are ventilated, he will cool off and start to listen.

An idea or a feeling can also be an emotional distraction. Until they are expressed, either through conversation or other actions, they are unfinished activities. Once expressed, the activity is complete and the emotional drive behind its expression subsides. Emotions such as anger can be diffused, through verbal expression, in the same way. A person who argues with you can be led through the expenditure of his anger.

You can listen to his point of view, encourage the expression of his anger and guide him through complete diffusion of the anger—all at the same time. Once the emotional feelings subside, he will feel no anxiety and will be less stereotyped in his thinking. As you probe and evaluate his position, he will become more and more willing to evaluate a new or opposing idea.

Often we encounter people who are not aware of the emotions their actions represent. A person who is constantly critical or who continues to grumble, complain or verbally abuse others may not be aware of the guilt, anxiety or anger he feels. Sometimes people employ these behaviors until they become habits. In either case, they should be made aware that their behavior indicates emotional distraction.

By simply stating to the other person that his grumbling or sarcasm makes you wonder if he is upset or angry about something, you will cause him to think about his feelings. If he is upset or angry he will become aware of it. You can then lead him through the expression and reduction of the anger.

If he is not upset or angry, he will at least see that his behavior is not consistent with his feelings. Some explanation should be forthcoming at this point. If he does not explain his behavior, you may ask for an explanation.

If he explains, for example, that he merely uses those expressions to make a point, you now have new leverage to use in getting your point across. You may, during the balance of the conversation, refer to such seemingly emotional expressions as his "point makers." This will keep him constantly aware of his behavior.

By showing concern for the other person, by demonstrating that you accept his emotions or his habitual way of making points, by keeping him aware of his feelings and expressions, by evaluating and responding to his ideas, you reduce his emotions and clear away the interference that keeps him from listening attentively to what you say.

The two steps that follow detail a method for using Psychological Leverage to reduce emotions and gain understanding. With these techniques you can develop a receptive climate and create an obligation on the part of the other person to listen to you.

How to Use the Acceptance Profile

The relief of anxiety, anger, or the other emotions requires the elimination of feelings of distrust, apprehension or hostility. These emotional feelings subside through understanding and supportive involvement. Feelings of distrust and hostility begin to dissipate when acceptance is demonstrated.

You can erase suspicions, build trust and relieve the other's anxiety simply by demonstrating acceptance. Acceptance permits the freedom to express oneself, to grow, to experiment and to develop. *One way to show acceptance is to verbally state that you understand the emotional tenseness he feels, and that the tenseness is quite natural for the circumstances.*

How to Use the Emotional Mirror

Psychologists have found that an emotion such as excitement or anger will peak out and then subside if allowed full expression. This can be done by using the passive listening technique, but a more effective method is to reflect the emotion verbally.

Reflecting an emotion is similar to reflecting an image from a mirror. In conversation you would use an allegorical two-way mirror. You let the message content pass through, but reflect the emotion back. In other words, you respond to the emotion only. This reflection of the emotion shows the other person that you understand and accept his actions. One way to demonstrate acceptance, show interest and gain information, all at the same time, is to use "reflective probing."

In *Effective Selling Through Psychology*, Dr. Buzzotta (1972) describes probing as showing interest in and respect for the other.

> Probes provide the support and encouragement so important to learning new ideas. Every probe implies in effect, "I want to hear more, I want to learn from you." Furthermore, every probe implies that the salesman *respects* the customer. It says, in effect, "Your opinion counts." Interest and respect are two of the basic elements of reinforcement. (P. 226.)

By demonstrating interest and respect, probing demonstrates acceptance. In addition, probing at the same time helps you learn the feeling and opinions of others. With this understanding, you can more easily deal with them. This understanding provides you with Psychological Leverage. It permits you to deal from a position of knowledge and this knowledge gives you power.

Examples of reflective probes are: "You seem to be angry, are you?" "Are you upset?" "I can see this bothers you. Are you angry about it?" In each case you relate to the emotion and not to the subject matter. The main purpose of using reflective probes is to demonstrate acceptance and to show the other person that you are listening and that you understand.

HOW ACTIVE LISTENING INDUCES CLEAR THINKING

This technique of responding to people's feelings has become known as "active listening." Dr. Carl Rogers (1957), the first to use the term, described "active listening" as "listening skills which *will help* employees gain a clearer understanding of their situations, take responsibility, and cooperate with each other." (P. 1.)

Dr. Rogers makes the point that listening need not be passive. By responding sensitively and probing to show interest, you are listening in an active way. Research clearly demonstrates that people undergo personality change and become more cooperative as a result of active listening. In a booklet entitled *Active Listening*, Dr. Rogers (1957) reports the conclusions of his clinical and research findings:

> When people are listened to sensitively, they tend to listen to themselves with more care and make clear exactly what they are feeling and thinking. Group members tend to listen more to each other, become less argumentative, more ready to incorporate other points of view. Because listening reduces the threat of having one's ideas criticized, the person is better able to see them for what they are, and is more likely to feel that his contributions are worthwhile. (P. 4.)

Passive listening permits emotions to subside, but active listening shows acceptance. You can demonstrate trust and acceptance by listening and responding to emotional interferences. Of course the way you respond is important. You build your Psychological Leverage not by what you say, but rather, by how you say it. If you use reflective probes, listen attentively and express understanding, your actions will have a dynamic effect on the other person.

The other person starts to trust you. He learns that you will not criticize his emotions. He then knows he can express his feelings and state his opinions freely. He can trust what you say because you have demonstrated trustworthiness during what to him are his most critical situations, periods of emotional disturbance.

You have the best chance of getting your own ideas accepted by someone who trusts you. The technique of active listening which promotes understanding, responsibility, cooperation and open-mindedness will gain this trust. Active listening will give you the Psychological Leverage necessary to gain real commitment to your ideas and instructions, from your subordinates and others.

How a Secretary Used Active Listening to Gain Psychological Leverage. When Nancy, a secretary who once worked for me, asked Gwen, one of her co-workers, to help with part of her work, Gwen replied, "No! I can't do my own work and everyone else's too." The clue that Gwen is upset is her reference to "everyone else's work." Nancy, recognizing that Gwen had some anxiety about doing extra work, used active listening to gain Gwen's cooperation.

Nancy: Has someone else given you his overflow?
Gwen: I'm always getting someone's overflow just before time to go home.
Nancy: Well, I can see that's upsetting you. [*Reflecting the emotion.*]
Gwen: It sure is. I take someone else's work and get stuck with it the next day and then can't finish my own work.
Nancy: You really are upset, aren't you? [*Reflecting emotion.*]
Gwen: Yes, I've had all I'm going to take.
Nancy: I can certainly understand your concern, if it's leading to your not getting your own work done. [*Acceptance.*] How often has this happened?
Gwen: Well, it only happened once, but I don't intend to let it happen again.
Nancy: I don't blame you. When did it happen? [*Acceptance.*]
Gwen: Just a few days ago. Joyce got behind and asked me to help her. She gave me a large stack of work at 4 P.M. The next thing I knew, she was gone and I had to finish her work and that put me behind with my own. My boss came in, saw all the work I had stacked up and thought I had been goofing off. That's why I don't want to take someone else's work late in the day.
Nancy: Well, no wonder. If I had had all that trouble I wouldn't either. I guess when we give our overflow to each other, we should hold it down to small parcels to be sure the person who helps us has time to finish it.
Gwen: Sure, that way we wouldn't have to worry about it interfering with our regular work. I wouldn't mind working on a small stack.
Nancy: Do you think you could help me tomorrow, if we do it that way? [*Using Psychological Leverage.*]
Gwen: Sure, I wouldn't mind that at all. As a matter of fact, I could help do one or two now, if you want me to.
Nancy: O.K., thanks a lot.

By probing, listening and showing acceptance, Nancy developed a listening climate. *She listened to Gwen and created an obligation for Gwen to listen in return.* Nancy developed trust and confidence by listening and probing. She showed concern for Gwen's anxiety, she did not criticize, and she helped Gwen relieve her anxiety. Gwen moved from her anxious state into a receptive one. This would not have been possible had Nancy argued with or criticized Gwen.

Listening without criticizing does not mean that you agree with what is being said. It simply means that you accept the person and recognize his right to his opinion. You respect him enough to listen to his opinion so that you can think about it and evaluate it. After you listen, think about and evaluate it, you may reject or accept part or all of what has been said. Remember, listening does not mean agreement.

If we look back at the interaction between Nancy and Gwen, we see that Nancy was a good listener. She never once said that she agreed with Gwen. She said she "could see it was upsetting," she could "understand" and she "didn't blame her." Nancy was helping Gwen ventilate her emotion. By giving Gwen understanding and encouragement, Nancy actually helped her talk out the anxiety and get the problem off her mind. She refrained from saying anything that would induce anger.

The more angry a person is the more venting will be required before the anger subsides. The angry person usually blows up and becomes very boisterous. He will probably raise his voice and perhaps use profanity. He'll make dictatorial, angry statements and top them off with, "No ifs, ands or buts."

Let's suppose a husband comes home from work four hours late. He added to that offense by neglecting to call his wife to tell her he would be late. With a ruined dinner and two or three hours of pacing the floor, it's not too hard to understand why the wife is angry. The minute her husband walks in the door, she will let him know how she feels.

The purpose of anger, according to Dr. H. S. Sullivan (1956) is "to destroy or drive away threatening or injurious situations." (Vol. 2, p. 96.) The wife's anger, in the above example, has built up because of the situation created by her husband. So the minute he walks in the door, she lets loose. In that release of anger, she relieves the feelings of anxiety, hostility and insecurity she has built up while waiting for her husband to come home.

In most cases when people are angry it can be traced to some irritating action of some other person. Either we ourselves or someone else did something to frustrate and cause feelings of insecurity in the other person. The problem is that most people don't realize they do things to anger others. Dr. Sullivan (1956) suggests the following approach when encountering an annoyed or angry person:

> Thus when another person seems annoyed or angry, we are most likely to approach an understanding of the situation if we ask ourselves whether what we did had in some way impaired his security, so that the anger was called out merely as an avoidance of the anxiety that would otherwise have been aroused. (Vol. 2, p. 96.)

Anger may require more probing than the other emotional states. Naturally, the more upset a person is the more difficult it will be for him to ventilate the emotion.

HOW TO USE REFLECTIVE PROBES

Reflective probes are especially useful to help ventilate emotions. While they are used to reflect or mirror back the emotion the other person is expressing, they also let the other person know that we understand their being upset. They are carefully worded so that they do not indicate agreement with what is being said.

By using reflective probes, in effect you separate the content of the message from the emotion. In so doing, you avoid the argument over facts or beliefs, you show your respect and acceptance for the other person, and at the same time you gain understanding and information about the other person's feelings. You also get the information he is basing his argument on, which can be used later to solve the problem or reach agreement. Your leverage increases with the increase in information.

Other examples of reflective probes are:

1. "I can see you are upset."
2. "You certainly are concerned about this, aren't you?"
3. "I understand how you feel; could you tell me more about it?"
4. "I don't blame you for being mad; could you give me the details on what happened?"

When the first reflective probe is used, the angry person will probably become more angry. This is the process by which ventilation takes place. Each reflective probe permits the other person to blow off a little more steam. Pretty soon all the steam has been blown off and the emotion is ventilated. Verbalizing the feeling seems to short-circuit the hostile behavior that might have resulted from the anger. The angry person is permitted to work out the aggressive feeling without resorting to physical violence.

In order to get the other person to listen, you must develop this atmosphere of trust and confidence. You avoid criticism of the other party to gain his confidence and show acceptance of him as a person to gain his trust. Once trust is established, you must avoid betraying that trust if you wish to retain a listening climate.

A listening climate is an open mental state. It is a climate that is conducive to accepting new ideas, a time when knowledge is sought. It is characterized by freedom of expression. Each person is free to express his own views and is sympathetic to the other's view. Each person is permitted complete leeway in expressing his idea, while the other listens attentively

How a West Coast Salesman Used Psychological Leverage to Talk Down an Order Cancellation. Chuck Gardner, an experienced salesman, told me how he used both passive and active listening techniques to save an order that one of his customers cancelled. Chuck said, "Ken is a very difficult customer. He seldom tells you what is on his mind. He is a very passive individual. I seldom know what I say that gets the order. Ken just says yes or no and there is very little discussion."

When Chuck called on Ken Biggs, the buyer for a small hardware chain, he found Ken in an unusually talkative mood. Ken made the same point over and over. He crowded his sentences together so tightly that Chuck could hardly keep up with what was being said. Ken elaborated on the problem he was having getting a sale put together. He mentioned a number of adverse consequences that were likely to occur due to improper follow-up.

Chuck said this was unusual behavior for Ken. He knew something was wrong. He knew Ken was often anxious and easily upset, so he listened passively, trying to determine the problem. Ken continued with rapid-fire statements, covering a number of problems and finishing with the statement, "I'll have to cancel the order I gave you last week for the new line of faucets." Chuck switched to active listening at this point, in an attempt to show acceptance and let Ken ventilate his emotions. The dialogue below approximately represents the conversation that took place between Chuck and Ken. I have taken the liberty of supplementing my memory to demonstrate the active listening technique.

Chuck: You seem very tense today, Ken, getting a sale set up must be really hectic. [Chuck used a reflective statement. He showed acceptance at the same time by implying it's O.K. to be tense when things are hectic.]

Ken: You bet I am. I spend half of my time setting up special sales so those guys out in the stores can make a profit. I do all the work here and I'm sick of following up on everyone else's work.

Chuck: With all that going on, I can understand your being upset. Did I do anything to cause any of the problem? [Chuck is still dealing with Ken's emotion. He shows understanding and gives Ken the opportunity to work out any feeling he may have about Chuck's part in the problem.]

Ken: I'm upset all right, and part of it is your fault. You were supposed to install the dump bins in each store to prepare for the new faucets. Here it is a week before the ad breaks and you still haven't done anything.

Chuck: How much of a problem has this caused you? [Chuck could have explained at this point that the dump bins were held up in Ken's warehouse. He chose instead to give Ken an opportunity to continue venting his emotion. At the same time Chuck gained information that helped save the sale.]

Ken: A big problem. If I ship this line of new faucets out to the stores and the dump bins are not set up, we'll have our storerooms filled all week. When I take a new item in and put it on sale, everything has to be perfectly timed. I'm just not going to purchase from a company that doesn't conform to the conditions we establish.

Chuck: If I understand you, the biggest problem is caused by the dump bins not getting to the stores. Is that correct? [Chuck sensed that Ken had ventilated his emotion and had cooled down. He summarized the problem to make sure his understanding of the problem was accurate.]

Ken: Yes, that sale is due to start next Thursday, and we want everything ready by Monday. We can't do that without dump bins.

Chuck: Ken, those dump bins are in your warehouse. They arrived yesterday, too late to go out to the stores on your trucks. I'm sorry I was unable to get word to you. I believe they will all be delivered to your stores by Monday. Will that give you time to set them up for the sale?

Ken: No. We want our product set up four to five days in advance. We like to give our customers time to become used to seeing the products in the store, prior to the sale.

Chuck: Ken, we have already shipped the faucets; they are going to be in your stores by Monday. Is there any way I could help or do anything to get the product displayed in time?

Ken: No, there just isn't time. I'm afraid we'll have to forget it for this week.

Chuck: Would you consider it for the following week? We could set up the dump bins Tuesday and Wednesday and the product would be on display for well over a week before the sale begins.

Ken   That would work. O.K., I'll try it. I want you to personally make sure every store has the product displayed by Wednesday.

By showing acceptance, employing active listening, and promoting ventilation, Chuck developed the Psychological Leverage to preserve the sale. Ken changed his buying practice as a result of the experience, and now orders well in advance of his sales.

3

The Psychology of Timing:
How It Can Double the Power
of What You Say

We often waste our words because our timing is off when we speak. Often people are preoccupied with other thoughts and activities and do not listen to the point you are trying to make. This problem can be overcome by watching and listening for tip-offs that indicate the other person's level of attentiveness.

In this chapter you will find out how to recognize the tip-offs that everyone gives all the time. You'll see how these tip-offs tell you when an individual is attentive and when he is inattentive. Some tip-offs are subtle and some are obvious. There are certain specific things people say that indicate interest and attention and others that indicate a closed or inattentive mind. You will learn, in this chapter, how to recognize and deal with these tip-offs.

By learning these tip-offs, you learn to deal with the psychology of the other person. You can use psychology based techniques to remove the preoccupations and emotional distractions that keep the other person from listening. You will be able to create the "right time" to make your point. We'll cover the tip-offs of inattentiveness first, then how to increase attentiveness and finally how to recognize when the other person is attentive and receptive to what you say.

FOUR TIP-OFFS THAT YOUR TIMING IS WRONG

When people are inattentive, they are not listening. Their receptivity to our words and ideas is very low. People give four types of clues that indicate a low level of receptivity or attentiveness. One is the use of "flat assertions" which often reflect the person's attempts to fulfill his ego needs for recognition. Secretiveness, the second clue, may reflect the individual's fears or need for security. Other activities, the third clue, may indicate boredom, the need to express his own views or that he is preoccupied with more pressing thoughts. The fourth clue is the expression of excitement or anger, reflecting an emotional distraction.

Recognizing and Dealing with the Assertive Shield

A flat assertion or a non-negotiable statement is often an assertive shield. It is used to keep you on the defensive. Such statements are presented as a fact rather than an opinion. Clues of this type, verbalized in authoritarian or non-negotiable statements, indicate that your timing is wrong. This type of assertive statement, made without consideration for the current needs or problems of others, is often a reflection of an ego need to demonstrate knowledge or power. It tells you the other person's receptivity is low, that he is shielding his mind from your comments.[1]

Examples of ego-related clues are encountered frequently in everyday life:

1. "I want it done my way."
2. "You are wrong."
3. "I'll make the decisions."
4. "My mind is made up."
5. "I've tried it before."
6. "I'm not interested."
7. "Skip the details."
8. "Do as you're told."
9. "This is the way it's going to be."
10. "I don't care about quality, just give me the price."

When you encounter a person who starts making flat assertions, you'll know that it would be poor timing to try to make a point. He will be inattentive and only listen at a superficial level. If he listens at all, he listens for points that he can refute. For better timing, wait for signs of higher receptivity.

Assessing and Dealing with Hidden Opposition

Secretiveness, the withholding of information, often indicates that the secretive individual is hiding his feelings of opposition. Another reason he fails to volunteer information is that he is suspicious. If the other person holds back information and forces you to develop your own facts, his level of receptivity is low and your timing is wrong.

In addition to withholding information the secretive person will try to be evasive and will avoid responding unless questioned directly. His answers will be characterized by "maybe," "I guess," "I suppose," and "Is that right?" He will attempt to avoid expressing his own opinion by pretending he doesn't know, doesn't have the knowledge, hasn't had time to check or is waiting for a report to be finished.

In a recent management seminar, one manager told me about a problem with one of his foremen. The foreman, we'll call him George, gave answers to the manager's questions that typify the secretive person's withholding of information. The conversation went like this:

Manager: George, how are things going?
George: O.K.
Manager: How's the production in your department?
George: O.K., I guess.
Manager: What can you tell me about your department?
George: We do our job.
Manager: Do you think we can improve the productivity in your department?
George: I don't know.
Manager: Suppose we buy new machinery, will that help?
George: I guess so.

George's unwillingness to volunteer any information, his refusal to evaluate his own department and his reluctance to respond to his boss's ideas, all indicate a low level of receptivity. George seems afraid to put himself out on a limb. He seems to be afraid that anything he says will generate trouble. These expressions of fear—secretiveness, suspicion, withholding information and reluctance to respond—are tip-offs to hidden opposition which indicates a low level of receptivity.

Examining Unrelated Activities

A clue indicating a low level of receptivity that is often overlooked is the other person's performance of unrelated activities. If you notice someone twiddling his fingers, pacing nervously, shuffling papers or looking away continually, he is not interested in what you are saying. These unrelated activities indicate a preoccupation with some problem or thought other than the one at hand.

Salesmen often encounter customers who read or continue their paperwork during the sales presentation. These are common "interferences" and are recognized by salesmen as obstacles that must be overcome if they are to make a sale. Some salesmen confront the problem directly by asking the customer if he needs time to finish. Others raise their voices or try to draw the customer's attention to samples or charts. Many give up in despair.

There are certain remarks that also indicate unrelated thought patterns. If you are discussing with your controller, for example, the placing of a new machine in the production plant and he introduces an unrelated remark, this is a clue to a low level of receptivity on his part. This actually did occur. Jim Grigg, a plant manager, called in his controller to discuss financing a packaging machine.

Jim: Carl, have you worked out the projected savings on the new
          packaging machine?
Carl: Yes, I have. I had quite a bit of trouble, however. I was not
          able to get any labor estimates from George, so I had to get
          estimates from engineering. It seems no one can ever get
          information from George, he's always too busy to help any-
          one else.

Carl's remarks about George, obviously are unrelated to the real purpose of this meeting which is to examine cost savings. These remarks indicate Carl is preoccupied with his own thoughts of resentment and irritation with George. If these feelings were not weighing on Carl's mind, he would have confined his remarks to the main topic of conversation suggested by Jim.

Unrelated remarks may be made about any topic that is pressing for expression. In the above example, Carl probably wants Jim to know that George is uncooperative. If Carl had been concerned about something else, say, making Jim aware of how accurate his work is or the long hours he works, his remarks would have reflected those ideas.

Carl might simply have felt the need to socialize a bit before talking business. In that case, he might bring sports, social events or some current news item into the conversation. Any unrelated topic, no matter how vague, is an indication of inattentiveness. If the remark seems inappropriate or unrelated in any way, the other person's receptivity is low and it is not the time to present your own point of view.

Listening for Expressions of Emotion

As discussed earlier, one way that emotions are expressed is through conversation. One of the emotions that is frequently expressed in this manner is anger. The verbalization of anger is an indication that your timing is off. This verbalization may include profanity, cutting remarks, yelling or a very cool and calm criticism. Whenever you encounter even mild criticism, you should recognize the situation as a "non-listening" one. You should be aware that the other person's receptivity will be low.

Flat assertions in an emotional tone can also indicate anger. Any form of emotionalism, anger, irritation, excitement or sarcasm, indicates a low level of receptivity. In our previous example, George's reaction to Carl's attempt to get the labor estimates for the new packaging machine is an example of low receptivity. Carl's timing was poor and he was ineffective in getting what he wanted.

Carl.   George I must have the labor estimates for operating the new packaging machine right away.
George   You always want everything right away. Well, I can't do it today.
Carl   I tell you, I have to have them today. My report is due to the boss at 9 A.M. tomorrow.
George.   I don't give a darn about your report.

When George expressed the first sarcasm, "You always want . . . ," he was showing a low level of receptivity. Carl might have recognized this as a low level of receptivity and dealt with it, but he did not. His next remark obviously intensified George's anger. George showed additional irritation with his reply, "I don't give a darn . . . "

All the indications of poor timing should be watched for and dealt with. *Each of them, flat assertions, secretiveness, unrelated activities and expressions of emotion, must be neutralized to improve your timing and develop the other person's receptivity to a level of interest, attentiveness and open-mindedness.*

DEVELOPING THE RIGHT PSYCHOLOGICAL TIME

The right psychological time occurs when the person we are attempting to persuade is open and receptive to our ideas. At this time his mind is free of the preoccupations and emotional distractions that characterize a low level of receptivity. His level of receptivity to our ideas and opinions is high. He will listen and evaluate what we say.

To utilize the psychology of timing, you must first recognize low levels of receptivity. These have been discussed in the previous two chapters. You must relate to the psychology of the other person, by showing *acceptance* and understanding for his emotions, feelings and actions. Finally, you must be willing to *probe* possible areas of distraction in order to help the other person ventilate his emotions.

This procedure will neutralize the obstacles that interfere with his attentiveness. It will raise his level of receptivity. When you probe and listen to him, you will create an obligation on his part to listen to you. He will be highly receptive at this time. This is the psychology of timing.[2]

How to Use the R.A.P. System

Recognition, acceptance and probing form a better way of "rapping." The "R.A.P." system is the only system that will always be effective in creating the "right" psychological time because it relates to the psychology of the other person.

By first recognizing (R) the emotional state of the other person you can determine his level of receptivity. By accepting (A) the other and his emotions you develop trust, and by probing (P) you permit the other to work out the "non-listening" emotional distractions and become receptive. Once you complete the R.A.P. sequence, you have developed the "right" psychological time.

In the "R.A.P." session, you help the other person ventilate or achieve completion by using appropriate questions that lead him through a satisfying explanation of his point of view. There are a number of different probes that can be used for this purpose.

The reflective probe is especially useful, as it draws out the emotions and feelings that accompany low levels of receptivity. By using reflective probes you allow the other person to vent his anger—blow his top—release his head of steam. Reflective probes show concern for and acceptance of the other's feelings and thereby you can gain his trust.

How a Secretary Used the R.A.P. System to Improve Relations with a Co-worker. For a practical example of the "R.A.P." system, I am again reminded of Nancy, the secretary who was familiar with experiments on "psychological timing," and tried to use them in her day-to-day relationships with the other secretaries. Once when given an especially heavy work load, she asked Gwen for help. Gwen replied, "No! I've had it today."

The curt answer was a clue that the other secretary was emotionally distracted. The worst thing (and the wrong thing) that Nancy could have done at this point would have been to say something sarcastic back to Gwen. If Nancy had become angry or had made a curt reply, the battle would have been on.

What chance is there that Nancy might have gotten help from anyone by arguing with him? None at all. The more we argue, the madder the other person gets, and the madder he gets the lower will be his level of receptivity. The lower the level of receptivity, the less listening will occur. To get the other person to listen, to use the "psychology of timing" we must raise their level of receptivity by using the "R.A.P." system.

Nancy recognized (R) the curt answer as an indication that Gwen was in the provoked state. She realized she had to do something to raise Gwen's receptivity or she would never get any help. To raise Gwen's receptivity, she must demonstrate acceptance (A), which she did through probing (P):

Nancy: Is something wrong?
Gwen: No, never mind.
Nancy: I can certainly see you are upset.
Gwen: You're darned right, I'm upset.
Nancy: Perhaps I can help. Would you like to tell me about it?

Nancy, who started out asking for help, has now herself offered help. By recognizing the curt "No" as a sign of emotional interference, Nancy took an approach that showed acceptance of Gwen, rather than getting involved in an argument.

If she were not aware that listening does not occur when a person is emotionally upset, she probably would have responded to the curt remark with sarcasm. She would have tried to convince, cajole, and finally belittle the other person in an attempt to force her to help. Naturally, none of those things would work. You can't win an argument with someone who isn't listening. This is the underlying basis for the "psychology of timing."

Nancy, by using three probes, did two things. She showed her interest and concern for the other party and she started gaining information, information that can be used in solving the problem. Once the reason for the refusal is determined, it can be logically discussed. This discussion, at a time when Gwen's receptivity has been increased, will probably lead to solving the problem and Nancy will get the help that she originally asked for. The conversation continued as follows:

Gwen: Yeah! I'll tell you about it. You sat there burning up the keys all morning while my boss was here. I had nothing to do and I could have helped you then. My boss would have seen me and given me credit for it. I saw him looking at you— burning up the keys—two or three times. You made me look bad. Now that the boss is gone, you want me to pitch in and do your work. Do you think I'm stupid or something?

Nancy: No, and I'm sure sorry if I gave you that impression. It's obvious that I've made a terrible mistake. I tried to catch up, by burning the keys, because I didn't think it would be fair to ask you for help if I could catch up on my own. I would have really appreciated the help this morning too. My boss gave me extra work this afternoon and I finally realized I couldn't catch up. That's why I was so late in asking for help. I certainly didn't mean to set a bad example. Is there anything I can do to make amends for this error?

Gwen: Well I guess I jumped too soon. I see now that you were just trying to get your job done. The next time, if you'll ask me in the morning I'll be glad to help.

Nancy had to wait until the next morning to get help, but she did get it. There was no argument, so bitter feelings were avoided. Nancy, by relating to the psychology of Gwen and by being courteous, developed a friendly atmosphere so that similar problems were more easily resolved thereafter.

When a person's level of receptivity is high, he will listen with an open mind. For a time, he will put his prejudices and preconceived opinions aside, listen to what you say and evaluate your ideas without trying to "shoot" them down. He may decide you're wrong, but he'll listen first. You can develop this highly receptive state by using the "R.A.P." system. That's how you develop the right "psychological time" to make your point.

When a person feels he is being attacked or provoked, when he is emotionally tense, when he is in an emotionally disturbed state, his level of receptivity is low. We can visualize the concept of "level of receptivity" by thinking of a see-saw. Visualize one end of the see-saw as the emotion and the other end as the level of receptivity. As the emotion goes up the level of receptivity goes down. As the emotion comes down the level of receptivity goes up. *Use the R.A.P. system to deal with a low level of receptivity.*

A Word of Caution

This system is meant to be used in everyday conversations. It is not meant as a technique for dealing with extreme irrationality or psychotic behavior. The habitually psychotic or irrational person is best avoided.

Sometimes the emotional tension has been caused by something that happened before we came into contact with the other person. Sometimes we do or say something that upsets the other person. Regardless of the cause, if the other person is upset, he will not listen. When you encounter a person who exhibits this emotionally distracting behavior, try to help him relieve his tension before pursuing your topic.

The Importance of Receptivity

The one most important concept in the "psychology of timing" is the concept of receptivity. We may learn all the rules of persuasion, but if we don't concentrate on "receptivity," all our efforts will be wasted.

Only when the other person's receptivity is high, is there any chance of getting your message across. You can determine the other person's receptivity by listening and probing. When he is in one of the "non-listening" states (low receptivity), he will make authoritarian or "non-negotiable" statements. He may also be rude or sarcastic.

When the other person is in a receptive state, he is willing to listen. At this point he may express some doubt or uncertainty, or he may ask questions or express approval. These are clues that your timing is right—he will listen. He still may not be willing to accept the idea, but at least he will listen.

Once you recognize a low level of receptivity, you may use the "R.A.P." system to raise the person's receptivity. By probing you can gain understanding of the other person's position. You can explore his evidence and determine the strength or validity of his argument. At the same time you show acceptance for his feelings and help him move into a receptive state. Then, when you understand his position, you may present your ideas with some chance of success.

You should refrain from presenting your ideas, however, until you have asked the other person to present evidence to substantiate his point of view. Explore his evidence with an open mind. If facts and logic support some of his views, indicate acceptance of that portion of his argument.

If some of his evidence is not valid, or if some point he makes is not supported by the evidence, you may relate your stronger evidence to refute those points.

The presentation of your evidence, however, should be made in a non-hostile manner. You must remember that arrogance or authoritative statements may irritate the other person. Once he becomes irritated, he is no longer in a receptive state and will no longer listen. You will be more successful if you present your evidence in a systematic manner at a time of high receptivity, without irritating the other person. That's the "psychology of timing."

THREE TIP-OFFS THAT YOUR TIMING IS RIGHT

When the other person is willing to listen to your ideas and opinions he is in a receptive state. One of the ways that he may indicate this willingness to listen is by expressing some doubt or uncertainty.

Recognizing "Incremental Uncertainty"

Such expressions as: "I'm not sure," "I don't know," "Maybe," "I don't think so," "I'm not certain," "I don't have the facts available," or "There seems to be something missing," are clues to a high level of receptivity. The person using these expressions is saying: "I don't have a fixed position on this subject, so I'm willing to listen to what you say about it." In other words his opposition has softened. If the softening occurred in stages or increments, it is called "incremental uncertainty." The greater the change toward uncertainty, the higher the level of receptivity. There are other clues that tell you that your timing is right. Buzzotta (1972) points out that *"questions for information, expressions of doubt and statements of approval all indicate a high level of receptivity."* (P. 217.)

Listening for "Segmented Approval"

Statements such as "that part looks good," "I think the idea is good," "Your product is good," "The machine looks nice," "I'm glad we're trying something new," "I'm happy with part of our results," are also indications that your timing is right.

Statements approving a segment or a part of what you say are very simply an indication that the person speaking has moved away from his previously stereotyped position. He agrees with some part of your argument and is receptive to more information on that particular point.

Suppose you are trying to convince the company president that you need a new plant that he opposes. If he indicates approval for the need for new machinery, you can use this area of receptivity as a further discussion point. You'll know you have his interest and can lead him from discussing machinery into discussing the new plant.

Responding to Questions That Indicate Good Timing

Sincere questions indicate a high level of receptivity. Questions such as: "You're the one who screwed it up, aren't you?" "You admit it's your fault, don't you?" or "You agree that I'm right, don't you?" are not questions for information. *Sarcastic* questions or questions asking you to "take the blame" indicate a low level of receptivity.

Questions asking for information are indications of a high level of receptivity and that your timing is good. You respond by answering the question and then presenting the point you want to make. Some examples of questions that indicate good timing are: "Will you give me more information?", "How does that work?", "When will it be complete?", "Why does this have to be done?", "How do I get the money back?" Those are a few samples of the many possible questions that might be asked, which indicate that your timing is right.

Now that we have a method developed for recognizing (R) the level of receptivity, if you put it to use, you will find people listening to you who never did before. When the level of receptivity is low, you need only let the person blow off the steam or talk the interfering situation (unfinished activity) to completion. Show acceptance (A) and probe (P) for information. In other words, R.A.P.

How a Hardware Salesman Used the R.A.P. System to Make a Sale. The R.A.P. system is a very effective tool for a salesman. When a salesman walks into a customer's office, he has no idea what problems he may run into. The customer may be preoccupied with a problem. That problem may or may not have anything to do with the current sales situation. No matter what the customer is preoccupied with, his receptivity will be low.

The customer's receptivity may also be low due to some anger-provoking situation. This anger may be the result of an interaction with another salesman, with some peer, a subordinate or with his boss. His anger may also be the result of something that happened with the product he last ordered from the salesman who just walked in.

Even when the other person is calm, he needs to be inspired to listen. You need to check his feelings, get his attention and capture his imagination. If you can find a topic that holds enough interest for him, he will be internally motivated to listen.

Paul, a hardware salesman, learned the R.A.P. system and tried it on a sales call. He walked into his customer's office, engaged in the usual initial friendly chatter and then attempted to establish a listening climate with his customer Ben.

Paul:	Ben, I have a promotional discount on coated hinges. How do you feel about using hinges as a promotional item?
Ben:	I wouldn't use your "damn" hinges on a bet.
Paul:	You seem to be angry.
Ben:	I "damn" sure am.
Paul:	I can see you are. Can you tell me what's wrong?
Ben:	Your 'damned' trucks were late with the last hinge order I gave you.
Paul:	I can certainly see why you are angry. How much of a problem did the late delivery cause you?
Ben:	I had two trucks going to stores that we only deliver once a week. The stores delivered by those trucks just didn't get any of your product last week.
Paul:	Do you have any other routes that you deliver only once a week?
Ben:	No. Just those two. But I want all orders on time.
Paul:	If I work out a method of getting the product here in time, and guarantee the delivery would you be interested in the promotion?
Ben:	Yes, I suppose I would. But I would have to be sure it got here before 8 A.M.
Paul:	Suppose I get the truck here a day early, would that solve the problem?
Ben:	No. We don't have room in the warehouse to store a truck load of hinges. We have our regular inventory to store and it's quite heavy now.
Paul:	Suppose I have the driver come in a day early. He can check in with you when he arrives. Then he'll come in at 8 A.M. the next morning.
Ben:	No. I don't trust those drivers. He'll just get drunk and oversleep the next morning. Then where will I be?

Paul: Suppose we have him leave his trailer at your dock over-
night. He can give you the key. If he isn't there at 8 A.M. you
open the trailer anyway.

Ben: O.K., maybe I'll try it that way. What's your deal?

Paul recognized the customer's low level of receptivity. Instead
of arguing with his customer, he showed acceptance for the
customer's feelings. He probed the customer's statements to gain
understanding. Instead of trying to prove the customer wrong, he
tried to work out a solution to the customer's problem, a solution that
the customer found acceptable.

The R.A.P. system will work in all situations between two people. If you want a co-worker, a subordinate or a boss to listen to you,
use the R.A.P. system. You may have difficulty using it the first few
times. It takes practice to learn any new skill. Practice with your
spouse, a friend, a child or a parent. Practice the system whenever you
can.

Remember the see-saw example. As emotions rise, the level of
receptivity goes down. When receptivity is low, you have a non-
listening climate. To raise the level of receptivity, you must help
people vent their emotions. You help them vent by probing. Probing
also elicits information from the other person. This information helps
you understand the other person's problems. This understanding
gives you a base from which you can present your ideas to the now
receptive person—at the right time.

Footnotes, Chapter 3

[1]V. R. Buzzota, Ph.D., R. E. Lefton, Ph.D., and Manuel Sherberg, Effective Selling
Through Psychology: Dimensional Sales and Sales Management Strategies. (New
York: Wiley Interscience, 1972), page 204.
[2]Ibid., page 16.

4

How to Gain Control by Boosting Your Psychological Impact on People

In order to strengthen your impact on people, you must determine your current impact, learn techniques to project an effective image and then practice those techniques. In this chapter you will, first, see how to evaluate your impact on others by observing their reactions to you.

You can improve your "impact quotient" by following a few simple steps that will enhance your image in the minds of other people. In this chapter you'll learn how to use words, actions, methods and emotions that translate into a positive psychological impact on people.

In this chapter you'll also see how to use the power of your "psychological impact" to improve cooperation from those with whom you interact in your daily life. These principles have been tested in hundreds of business situations and found successful. They have been used by parents in dealing with children and by husbands and wives. They work, and you can use them in your everyday conversations and activities.

FOUR WAYS TO MEASURE YOUR "IMPACT QUOTIENT"

You can use one or both of the following techniques to determine your current impact on others.

Seek Feedback to Measure Your Impact

The most obvious way to get feedback is to ask for it. Ask someone you work with to evaluate your impact on others. Ask him to listen to a conversation between you and a subordinate or peer and then give you his opinion on the impact you had on the other person. He may report, after the listening session, that you were too easy or too harsh. He may point out specific places where the things you say are working against the objectives you are trying to accomplish.

I used this procedure once during a review session with a product department head. The department head had consistently refused to follow my instructions in the handling of direct sales. My instructions were that the shipment was to go from the manufacturing plant directly to the purchaser without intervening storage.

I asked a peer to sit in as a critical observer, while I reviewed this subordinate's performance. The peer was to listen carefully and try to determine the impact my remarks made on the subordinate. He would discuss his observations with me privately after the review meeting was concluded.

During the review, I tried to listen to the reasons the product manager gave for not following my instructions. Often he had sales, he said, that did not fill the truck. He had to fill the truck in order to get the lowest freight rate. In order to fill the truck, he would purchase product that was not sold and upon arrival, place the unsold product in storage in a public warehouse. I told him I understood the problem of filling the truck, but insisted that in the future he must avoid storing product in public storage.

After the review my critical observer gave me his impression. He pointed out that I had a negative impact upon the subordinate. He doubted that the problem had been solved at all. I had, in his opinion, left an impression that I was only interested in getting my own way. He felt I had missed an opportunity to explore the costs involved in the storage system, and he believed that by comparing costs of the two systems I could have gained understanding and commitment from the subordinate.

Use the "Question-Response" Yardstick

Another way to seek feedback is to specifically ask the person you are dealing with. When discussing a problem with a subordinate, you can say: "What do you think?", "How will that work?", "Will what I've said cause you any problems?", "What obstacles do you see?", "Is there any problem with what I've said?"

Many people are reluctant to tell you that you are having a negative impact upon them. But most people will, when asked, give you their opinion on problems or obstacles that you are introducing. You can analyze those responses to determine your impact quotient.

Use the "Non-Verbal Observation" Yardstick

You can also learn a great deal about your impact by watching and listening to others. If the other person responds warmly and enthusiastically, you may assume your impact to be positive. If the other person seems to be reluctant to talk, if he grimaces, makes subtle objections or is openly argumentative, you will know your impact is negative. It may develop that there are other reasons for these reactions, but generally they are influenced by your behavior.

The mere fact that you start observing other people's non-verbal behavior will help you strengthen your impact. If you watch closely, you will detect irritation, nervousness, preoccupation, and lack of commitment. The longer you observe, the more aware you will become of the subtle clues people give to indicate their feelings.

Once aware of these clues, you can direct comments and questions to the problem area. Let's suppose a manager is talking to a foreman. He is telling the foreman he needs overtime worked to meet the production budget. He notices the foreman's face drop. He seems to be provoked at having to work overtime. The manager asks questions and finds the foreman has a personal problem that needs immediate attention. If the manager had not been watching non-verbal behavior, if he had not been seeking feedback, he might have missed the clue. He would then have missed the opportunity to improve his impact on the foreman.

Evaluate Your "Cooperation Index"

When you ask your subordinates to work overtime or to increase production to meet a deadline, you have an opportunity to check your impact quotient. If you get the increased production, your impact is positive, if not, it may indicate a negative impact. The willingness of your subordinates to cooperate is a valuable indication of your impact on others.

You can evaluate the cooperation of your peers as another indication of your impact quotient. If your peers are constantly finding excuses not to give you needed help, this may indicate a reluctance to cooperate with you. If your requests are often denied, even when you can see that there is no reason for their denial, this strongly implies a negative impact.

You can also evaluate your relationship with your superiors. If you are given the necessary support you require to carry out your assignments, this cooperation indicates a positive impact. If your superiors cooperate by approving your recommendations, providing financial or other support, your impact quotient is obviously positive.

You may also get an indication of your impact on people by evaluating the cooperation you get from your family, friends and neighbors. Form the habit of evaluating the cooperation you get from people to determine your "impact quotient "

THREE WAYS TO IMPROVE YOUR "IMPACT QUOTIENT"

You can improve your impact on others. You can break through defensiveness, rationalization, multiple objections, inattention, aggressiveness and unresponsiveness. You can gain control in conversation, develop cooperation from others and build morale by using in everyday situations techniques developed by psychologists for professional counselling.

How to Use the "Discussion-Time-Phase" Technique to Gain Control

Often in conversation, we find that understanding is blocked due to the defensiveness or aggressiveness expressed by subordi nates. Others may constantly veer away from the purpose of the conversation or fail to respond in a constructive way. You can gain control when confronted with these non-productive behaviors by using the "Discussion-Time-Phase" technique.

The "time-phase" is a pause to permit the other person time to absorb your comments, freedom to respond to each comment separately and the freedom to express his feelings as well as his ideas. The "Discussion-Time-Phase" technique builds an obligation on the part of the other person to listen open-mindedly to you. Your behavior, over time, will have such an impact on the other person as to influence him to actually copy your behavior. This leads to understanding.

The first technique then, for improving your impact on others, is simply to *pause after you make a comment, to give the other time to absorb what you have said.* If your comment is a new or novel idea, a longer pause will be required. The more complex the comment the more time the other will need to absorb and integrate the idea into his own mind.

A study conducted by the U.S. Navy showed that when a lecturer provided pauses, the participants remembered 58 percent of the material Groups given the lectures without pauses under the same conditions, remembered only 37 percent of the material. The groups which were given pauses utilized the time to do something with the new material. They took notes or thought about the content; they integrated it into their own thinking.

In conversation you can do the same thing the Navy did. You can allow time for subordinates or others to integrate or do something with your comments. Even though they will not always accept them, if given time to think about them, they may understand them.

How to Use "transitional Questioning" to Control the Conversation

A second technique for strengthening your impact on others is to employ "Transitional Questioning" to control the conversation. There are three main categories of questions, each of which accomplishes a different purpose: The three categories are convergent, divergent and evaluative.

1. Convergent questions pull the conversation toward a specific point.
2. Divergent questions pull the conversation toward a general area.
3. Evaluative questions open the conversation to feelings and opinions.

Convergent questions draw the other's thinking toward a specific conclusion. They are used to pull bits of information from a wide background and collate these bits together as they relate to a specific topic. Convergent questions bring the facts from various sources together in the formation of a pattern or a conclusion. For example, we might draw out through questioning, legal, moral, religious and economic principles that relate to unemployment. We would then converge these principles into a proposal for dealing with unemployment.

Divergent questions are used to get the same result as convergent questions; but they are used to lead the other from a specific conclusion to a generalization. This generalization is then shown to cover the problem of current concern. Divergent questions direct the interpretation or the translation from the generalized whole or pattern to a specific application.

Evaluative questions, the third category, are the most useful in two-way discussion. Evaluative questions give the other person the freedom to state his opinions. With those opinions often come feelings, doubts and concerns which provide the basis for discussion that will lead to understanding.

You can pre-plan questions that will improve your impact on your subordinates in every interaction. You can initiate, guide and direct the course of the conversation with these "Transitional Questions." You can elicit information that will simplify getting the job done, deciding between alternatives and making decisions.

Questioning not only gives you control over the conversation, it gives you the understanding necessary to make better decisions. In *New Patterns of Management*, Rensis Likert (1961) reported that 95 percent of the foremen questioned in his study thought they understood their men's problems well. In answering the same question, 66 percent of the subordinates said the foremen did not understand. Questioning will resolve this problem.

A thorough understanding of the situation cannot be accomplished with one question. You need to ask questions to determine the facts and ask for reasons to explain the facts. Then you ask for the feelings or opinions of the subordinate or other person about the situation. You might first ask, "What is the problem?" then, "What caused this?" or "Why is it a problem?" and then ask, "How do you feel about this problem?" or "What is your opinion of the problem?" These questions will provide a background of information that will give you the understanding that many subordinates say management doesn't have.

Questioning techniques work well because people generally provide answers to protect their own image of themselves. Many people have an ego-related fear that if they don't know some bit of information, they will be thought of as "not in on what's going on." Others fear being thought secretive or deceitful. People also have a biological drive to complete each situation. For these three reasons, people will generally give you the answers you need, especially if you explain why you need the information.

How to Time Your Presentation for Maximum Impact

A third technique in strengthening your impact through two-way discussion is to time the presentation of your comments or opinions to coincide with a receptive period of the subordinate or other person. As discussed previously, the other person will show this receptivity by asking questions, expressing doubts or showing some form of approval.[1]

Psychologists tell us that people tend not to hear, clearly enough to understand or remember, messages with which they disagree. If the other person expresses any disagreement, then you are facing a more difficult task. The best approach is, after thorough questioning, to build up a receptive state, to solicit the other's opinion on each comment you make. This will help make sure he understands what you have said.

You will be able to gain commitment to your decisions if you can develop this understanding. Even if the subordinate disagrees with your decision, if he understands your reasons and your goals, he will be more likely to do what you want. This understanding creates an obligation to follow your instructions and eliminates the possibility of excuses due to a lack of understanding.

FOUR WAYS TO USE YOUR "PSYCHOLOGICAL IMPACT" TO IMPROVE COOPERATION FROM PEOPLE

You can get better results, increase the power of your words, expand your influence and gain cooperation from people by using your "Psychological Impact" in a constructive way. "Active Listening," "Feedback Contingency," "Monitored Freedom" and "Environmental Monitoring" are four techniques that you can use to develop cooperation from others.

The Principles and Techniques of "Active Listening"

The basic technique used by Dr. Rogers to gain cooperation from others was *active listening*. Dr. Rogers (1957) found that people who were listened to carefully and sensitively began to clarify their own thoughts and attempted to present them more clearly. The fact that someone really cared about what they had to say caused them to think carefully when speaking.

Since there was no threat or criticism, people who were listened to began to open up more, became more cooperative and began to follow the example set by the listener. And they began to listen more themselves.

You can use active listening to gain cooperation from your subordinates, peers and superiors. The basic success of active listening is due to its orientation toward the other person. When you listen carefully to another person you are showing respect for that person. You are also showing concern for him. One way to show that you have listened to a person is to relate back to something this person has said in the past.

You might start your program of active listening by listening for some specific thing that seems important to the other person. Make a mental note of this and then you can question or comment on it from time to time to show the other person you are concerned enough about his problems to remember them.

The purpose of active listening is to remove barriers that cause defensiveness in others; to provide psychological safety for others; to encourage them to express their feelings and opinions openly; to encourage them to listen to and evaluate others' ideas; and to encourage their cooperation.

Active listening requires that we avoid passing judgement. The avoidance of criticism will provide the atmosphere conducive to cooperation. If there is no criticism there is no reason for defensiveness or argumentativeness.

The following steps, based on Dr. Rogers' recommendations, have been developed and tested in business and social situations. These nine steps, after extensive testing, have been revised and made applicable to all situations. Cooperation can be gained by managers from their subordinates, by salesmen from their customers, by parents from their children or by anyone who practices the nine steps in his everyday activities.

NINE STEPS FOR ACTIVE LISTENING TO GET COOPERATION FROM EVERYONE

1. Listen for clues to emotional distractions as well as comments relevant to the discussion.
2. Respond to the emotion by using reflective statements or probes. Let the other person know that you accept and understand his feelings.
3. Show you are listening by responding to irrelevant remarks.
4. Listen carefully, without interrupting, to show respect for the other person's ideas and opinions.
5. Watch for non-verbal clues to determine the other person's level of receptivity.
6. Test for understanding by using summary statements and asking questions to clarify the other's position. The use of summary statements also shows respect. It shows you respect the other enough to pay attention to what he says.
7. Express your own feelings freely and genuinely when the other person is receptive. Be honest in your opinion even though it may clash with the opinion of the other person.
8. Pause after you express your opinion, so the other person will have time to evaluate it.
9. If the other person does not respond to your statement, ask a question to determine whether or not he understood your opinion.

Using the "Feedback Contingency" Concept

Whether or not people change their behavior is contingent upon the feedback they get. You can gain more cooperation by providing feedback that shows them the value of cooperation. One way of doing this is to provide a model of cooperative behavior where positive results can be seen. This is one way of using the "Feedback Contingency" concept.

Humans continue into adulthood their childhood practice of patterning their behavior after significant adults. As adults, however, they are more selective in the acquisition of patterns and are more subtle in expressing them. The patterning, however subtle, encompasses all behavior that seems to them to be effective.

The selection of the significant other is related to the success or impact this person has on those with whom he interacts. The most significant behaviors will be assimilated and utilized by those subordinates who see the behavior as being successful.

You can gain cooperation from others by demonstrating the usefulness of cooperation. By cooperating with others in plain view of your subordinates, you provide a pattern for them to assimilate into their own behavior.

Providing accurate feedback to subordinates gives them the information necessary for their motivation. It has been proven over and over again that employees at all levels will improve their performance, once they become aware that their results are lower than expected.

If you show your subordinates the gap between their actual performance and the goal they are expected to achieve, and then provide daily or weekly feedback, their performance will improve more rapidly than you may think possible.

If you are dealing with production employees, for example, and your goal is 100 units per hour, you must first make the goal known. Then post daily production figures, so that the workers can see the gap between where they are and where they should be. The goal-striving psychology of each of them will motivate them to reach the goal. Unless there are mitigating problems, you should see major improvement within five to six weeks.

Applying the "Monitored Freedom" Concept

A third technique in gaining cooperation from others is to *help them satisfy their physical and ego needs.* Psychologists tell us that the frustration of physical needs results in anger and hostility. The ego needs grow out of this same frustration. The person whose physical needs are frustrated, develops the ego-related need for power, freedom and knowledge which can be used in the satisfaction of the physical needs.

By gaining power and freedom from the dependency of others, the physical needs are not likely to be frustrated by others. The primary reason for the development of the ego-needs then is to avoid the frustrations resulting from having others block the physical needs.

In the work situation, you can provide this feeling of freedom simply by giving each subordinate an opportunity to speak freely or have the freedom to participate in improving his job. Personal conversations and written suggestions both offer the subordinate the freedom to have an impact on his job. Give him this freedom and make him aware that you are purposely doing it.

A person who realizes that his observations and ideas will be listened to is more likely to be cooperative. His esteem needs for freedom and recognition are being fulfilled. Consequently there is no frustration. When there is no frustration, instead of anger there will be a warmer feeling leading to cooperation.

Using the "Environmental Monitoring" Concept

A fourth technique that insures cooperation is to *provide a predictable environment for your subordinates.* People need to know that they will be treated fairly, receive social and financial rewards for good work and that these conditions will remain stable. No man can please a superior who changes the rules each day. Just as uncertainty breeds resistance, predictability breeds cooperation. Monitor these environmental factors on a regular basis and keep the environment predictable.

A TEN-POINT GUIDE TO PRACTICAL APPLICATION

The following ten points offer an effective guideline for developing a highly productive group of subordinates with high morale who will be highly cooperative.

1. Group your subordinate staff and supervisory personnel into three- to seven-man teams. You may have more than seven men on one team depending upon organizational structure or the number of divisions you are dealing with. For example, you might have nine

divisions, in which case you would work with the nine division managers as one team.

Never form teams of less than three people. Two will, in most situations, not be an effective problem-solving team. Leave production personnel in complete production units regardless of the number. Salesmen should be left in groups conforming to their organizational grouping also. A supervisor with more than twelve or fourteen salesmen should consider breaking them into two groups for discussion and problem solving sessions.

2. Train all management or supervisory personnel to measure and improve their Impact Quotient. They should listen patiently to their employees, not become emotionally involved, provide feedback without criticism, protect the subordinates' dignity, support the employees with advice, help and training, learn the employees' needs and offer guidance that will help them fulfill those needs. Use the Active Listening technique to win their trust and confidence.

3. Develop a high team spirit with each team. Make each team member feel that he is a member of an elite group with special skills, that he is better trained and more highly skilled than his counterparts in other companies.

4. Provide a feedback method to measure their achievements that makes them look good as they progress. Look for positive aspects to emphasize and relate to mistakes as a part of the learning process.

5. Hold team meetings often. Provide for social contact so that the formal and informal organization is the same. Don't expect too much from the first few meetings. In the early stages, many expressions of feelings and irrelevant remarks will be made. Hidden "agendas" will impede progress and work against cooperation. Later, when these feelings have been aired and specific goals have been established, more progress will be made, more cooperation will evolve.

6. Constantly work toward improving working conditions. Try to satisfy as many as possible of the subordinates' physical needs. Increase salary, fringe benefits and working conditions. Monitor the environment and try to keep it predictable. Apply company policy fairly.

7. Enhance each subordinate's self-image. Ask for his opinions, remember and comment on things that are important to him, let him know you consider him a professional, let him know in every way that his personal dignity and self-esteem are important to you. Practice Active Listening, provide for the freedom of self-expression.

8. Keep communications open in both directions. Provide spe-

cific goals and problems for team meetings. Ask for feedback from individual members of each team.

9. Make certain the goals are obtainable. Let the team members participate in goal setting.

10. Make training programs available so that each employee can attain the highest possible level of proficiency.

Footnote, Chapter 4

[1]V. R. Buzzota, Ph.D., R. E. Lefton, Ph.D., and Manuel Sherberg, Effective Selling Through Psychology: Dimensional Sales and Sales Management Strategies. (New York: Wiley Interscience, 1972), page 204.

5

How to Use Psychological Leverage to Resolve Conflicts and Get Things Done

As a group leader or manager you are exposed to two common sources of conflict. One is conflict between two people for whom you are responsible, and the second is conflict that develops between you and one other person. The other person may be someone subordinate to you or someone who holds a higher position than you.

This chapter will provide techniques that will resolve either of the two forms of conflict. You'll see how, in both cases, to relate to the psychology of the other person. You will see how to use "Psychological Leverage" to resolve conflict that often arises from valid differences of opinion relating to facts, methods or values. By eliminating conflict you will get more productivity from everyone.

Techniques developed by psychologists that have been used successfully in business to reduce ego-related conflicts are also explained. You can use these field-tested techniques to divert people away from aggressive actions and direct them toward more constructive goals.

You will also be able to use the techniques covered in this chapter to develop Psychological Leverage in dealing with individuals who are driven by the desire for power, prestige and autonomy. You will learn to get things done in a constructive and creative way by using psychological techniques to neutralize the conflict that may arise from these personal drives.

THREE TYPES OF REACTIONS THAT INDICATE CONFLICT

People react in three different ways when they feel in conflict with someone else. They will openly oppose, hide their opposition or agree with the other person in a superficial way. You can gain insight into the psychology of the other person by learning to recognize the difference in these three reactions. This insight will provide you with the "Psychological Leverage" necessary to get the best results from each of these different types of people.

Open Opposition

Disagreements based on individual differences of opinion can be dealt with by utilizing logical facts related to the common overriding goal of both parties. If the conflict is not related to values or ego-needs, logic will reduce the conflict. This method of discussion appeals to each person's need for rationality.

Superimposed over these rational statements of opposition, we often find expressions of anger or expressions of arrogance designed to satisfy ego-needs. Understanding how these statements relate to each person's needs results in Psychological Leverage. This leverage, which relates to the psychology of the other person, is the critical element in resolving conflicts that hinder results.

A person who is driven by power needs will express his opposition with statements that enhance his power. One of his favorite techniques for dealing with conflict may be to give orders. He may say: "This is how I want you to settle the problem." Another method this person may use to fulfill his need for power is to monopolize the conversation. His need for power may be expressed by making threats, arguing that "it has to be done immediately," and by referring to rules, regulations and policy which support his authority.

The need for recognition is also expressed, often unconsciously, through statements of opposition. The individual may want recognition for his knowledge, skills, experience or position. Statements such as: "I've been doing it this way for years," "This is based on scientific principles," or "It's up to me to make the decisions," are typical attempts to gain recognition and status.

Statements of opposition such as: "I've already made the decision," "I'll work it out," "This is my problem" or "I can solve this alone," are attempts to satisfy this person's need for independence and autonomy.

Prestige and authority fill out this group of ego-related needs and are also expressed through statements of opposition. A person seeking prestige will relate to his authority, to rules, regulations and company policy as a means of opposition. He will use references to his past positions and successes in his arguments.

By listening carefully to people in a conflict situation, you can determine when those ego-related needs are operating. You can then work toward a solution that does not frustrate the needs of either person. By relating to the psychology of each individual you develop the leverage necessary to gain commitment to a rational solution to the problem.

Hidden Opposition

The fact that people often hide feelings and opinions makes it difficult to recognize conflict. Hidden opposition creates a management problem because this person's opposition will affect productivity. He keeps his opinion hidden in order to avoid conflict but in the process internalizes his anger (turns his anger inwardly). The result is resentment and a lack of cooperation.

The internalized anger also creates pressures on the individual. He seems to be driven to make his reservations known in a way that does not get him in trouble. Often this person will make mild or subtle comments in relation to some aspect of the area of disagreement. He may say something like "That seems a little out of place," or "It looks like it's possible to have a problem there."

In his relationships with management, this type of person feels insecure. The insecurity or lack of trust causes him to feel tension. He is uncertain about the outcome of his actions and feels insecure because of what he perceives as an unstable environment.

In resolving conflicts between people of this type, you can relate to their need for stability and trust. You can use the previously discussed "active listening" and "probing" techniques to penetrate the secretiveness that surrounds this internalized anger. These techniques are especially useful in releasing internalized anger and promoting trust.

In establishing trust it is important that each person be allowed to keep the private areas of his life secret. Probing should be directed at the expression of mild or subtle concern that the individual has expressed. This way you are relating to something he brought up. If he feels his privacy is being invaded, tension will appear again and interfere with the open discussion.

How Conflict Between Two Managers Resulted in a Lost Order. One afternoon the branch manager of a West Coast manufacturer received a call from one of their most important customers. The customer had not received his Monday order, had called in Tuesday and was assured his order would be delivered Wednesday. Now it was Thursday and his order still had not arrived.

When the branch manager began his investigation to determine why the order had not been shipped, he heard one division manager say, "That's typical of Paul (the division manager responsible for the sale of the missing order), he's always having problems with his orders."

This subtly sarcastic remark about Paul led the branch manager to the discovery of the missing order. The branch manager probed the remark and slowly pieced together what had happened.

Paul had left town on a hurried business trip Monday and had forgotten to enter the shipping order in question. Since Paul constantly forgot to place his orders when under time pressure, the other employees resented correcting his errors. When the customer called in Tuesday, the order was referred to a division head for approval. The division head purposely withheld the order to teach Paul a lesson.

By probing and using "active listening" techniques the branch manager solved his problem. He found the missing order and had it shipped, but more importantly he found the cause of a problem. He was then able to begin working with the division managers to reduce the conflict between them.

Superficial Agreement

Often, people are so motivated to fulfill their need for group or individual approval, that they become insincere and establish a false front in which they superficially agree with everything you say, rather than take the chance of losing your approval.

These people are especially adept at internalizing anger. They feel they have to hold their anger in check in order to keep people's approval. They are very careful not to let their angry feelings be seen. The tip-off to superficial agreement is the immediate acceptance of everything that is said. The fact that they do no questioning for understanding and offer no differing opinions is a signal that their agreement is superficial.

When dealing with superficial agreement, you can determine whether or not there is underlying anger or disagreement by probing. You can ask for specific details on how they will carry out the assignment. Often in discussing these details, the individual will let his guard down and reveal his disagreement. By asking for any problems they might expect to encounter, you may also be able to determine what anger or resistances they hold.

A Branch Manager Who Missed the Signs of Conflict. A new manager at a West Coast branch office was fooled into thinking that the organization was one big happy family. There was a lot of joking intertwined with what seemed to be friendly sarcasm among his employees. This subtle sarcasm turned out to be a clue to a deep-seated, long-simmering, internalized anger.

Over the years a deep hatred had developed among four division managers. They were competitive with each other, but any two or three might team up against the others. The new branch manager missed seeing these signs of conflict because of the overly agreeable nature of his employees.

One afternoon the branch manager walked into the office to find the three managers embroiled in bitter argument. Two of them were teamed up against the other, and their abusive remarks and loud voices had drawn the attention and stopped the work of all other employees.

The branch manager stopped the argument by asking the three division managers to come into his office so that he might help them solve the problem. By getting the managers into his office, he took them out of the sight and sound of the other employees. This gave the branch manager Psychological Leverage as he removed the protagonist's need for holding a position just to satisfy his ego in front of the other employees.

As soon as they were all seated in the office, the three division managers reverted to their overly agreeable nature and tried to say "yes sir" to the branch manager's every suggestion. But he wasn't fooled this time. He asked questions and insisted on answers. He learned of the long-standing bitterness between the managers and asked them to start working on overcoming their differences.

In order to insure success, he questioned them about the specific steps they would take, when they would begin and what they would do when they ran into problems. He then informed them that they were to come into his office at any time they could not reach agreement without argument. They were then sent back to their jobs.

Over the next year, one of the four quit and the other three began to work better together. The branch manager watched for signs of hidden opposition and was successful in neutralizing future conflict before it exploded.

A FIVE-STEP PLAN TO RESOLVE CONFLICT

You can follow these five steps in resolving conflict between subordinate groups of two or more people. The same techniques apply in one-on-one confrontations that you may have with a single subordinate, peer or superior. When dealing with groups, you may have to separate them and deal with each one individually. By dealing privately with each one, you are in a better position to explore his opinions and let him ventilate his negative emotions.

The two critical elements in resolving conflict are (1) providing an opportunity for each person to express his emotional feelings, and (2) the development of a solution that does not frustrate the psychological needs of either person. The opportunity for expression of emotional feelings may be provided in a group or it may be provided separately and privately. Once these two critical psychological elements are considered, you will be able to synthesize all the available information into a work-related solution. The following five steps will satisfy these two critical elements:

1. Begin with a neutral approach.
2. Examine the other person's psychological position.
3. Use the leverage of your position.
4. Use the psychology of suggestion.
5. Use psychological principles to establish a solution.

Begin with a Neutral Approach

To resolve conflict you need information. If you take a neutral position, people will feel free to provide the information you need. But if you indicate in any way that you have taken a pre-established position, they may hide their facts and opinions.

Remember, your purpose in the first step of conflict-resolution is to gather information. If you listen carefully each individual will tell you his needs. Once you understand these needs, you'll be in a position to deal with them.

Each person will speak more freely, provide more information and think more clearly in an atmosphere of acceptance. As he thinks more clearly, he will begin to offer solutions that are pertinent to the real problem, rather than concentrating on his need for emotional release or self-esteem. Although it is important to get ideas on resolving the conflict from those participating in the conflict, it is equally important that you refrain from pressuring or trying to force ideas from the individual. If you provide the proper atmosphere, each person will eventually offer his ideas and opinions without pressure. Active Listening will help establish this atmosphere.

Why You Should Avoid "Negotiating" Conflicts. Make certain that each individual knows that you are there to gain information, not to negotiate. Negotiation, at its best, leads to a compromise that may be workable but ignores the feelings and ego-needs of those involved in the conflict. At its worst, negotiation identifies losers. Losers will not be committed to the changes or solutions and the conflict will soon superimpose itself over some new problem. The negotiation process, if used, will again be concentrated on the work problem and ignore the psychological factors that are so important to your continued effectiveness.

One way to uncover psychological factors is through self-disclosure. Self-disclosure of feelings, doubts and concerns tends to evoke similar disclosures from other people. You can relate experiences or feelings of your own, without taking a position on the current issue. The other individual will then disclose his feelings to you. In this manner you can determine the individual's ego-related needs. Once you are aware of these needs, you will be able to see how the current work problem affects these needs.

If you can uncover solutions to the work problem that remove the threat to the fulfillment of each individual's needs, your resolution of the conflict will be permanent and productive. Sometimes the work problem is simple to correct, but some additional change must be made to satisfy the ego-needs of the people involved. Develop this additional change and present it as part of the total resolution. This will insure against the conflict reappearing over some other trivial matter.

Examine the Other Person's Psychological Position

The second step, examining the other person's psychological position, tells you how important or how significant the problem is to each individual. If an individual feels the problem is a relatively unimportant one, he may readily agree to whatever solution is offered. If he sees the problem as one that is highly significant or important, then you can expect firm resistance to any solution that does not measure up to his expectations.

The importance each person places on a problem will be related to how the problem impinges upon his psychological needs. There are, again, three areas that the problem may affect:

1. The way the problem relates to each person's freedom to do his job. If the problem concerns restrictions that hamper a person in performing his task, he may fear that the restriction will cause him to appear incompetent.
2. The restriction the problem places on each person's freedom to express himself. This restriction may create the fear of not being able to protect his interest through conversation.
3. The most critical, and most often overlooked, is the issue of restrictions or obstacles the problem places on a person's attempts to satisfy his psychological needs. If a person's attempt to gain recognition, status, approval or security are restricted due to some element of the problem, the solution will have very little chance of succeeding.

A Federal Experiment in Structured Conflict Resolution. An agency of the federal government conducted a number of experiments in which various techniques were used in an attempt to remove conflict from groups who were meeting to solve governmental problems. In one meeting, typical of the structured approach to resolving conflict, the group members were required to:

1. "Figuratively" sign a contract agreeing to limit their remarks to ideas pertaining to the problem.
2. Refrain from arguing with other members of the group.
3. Work consciously toward the solution of a specific problem.

This meeting, as well as many similar ones, was unproductive. Everyone seemed to hold back and no fruitful ideas were developed to solve the problem. The system failed.

The failure of the structured approach is due to the exclusion of psychological factors. The structure which prohibits argument and requires that all remarks be limited to the problem, blocks the group members' psychological needs and results in internalized anger. This blockage of psychological needs interferes with creative thinking and works against the problem being solved.

Use the Leverage of Your Position

When dealing with subordinates you have a unique edge in resolving conflict. You have the power to satisfy most of your subordinates' needs due to your managerial position. This power gives you additional leverage in resolving conflict. You can use this leverage to insure that the solutions arrived at are solutions that will be effective in getting the job done. The use of this leverage is the third step in conflict resolution.

You can insure each group member the freedom of space required for his activities and the psychological space for the free expression of the ideas that he requires to fulfill his personal needs. Your positional power enables you to protect each person so that he is not belittled by other members of the group. This eliminates tension and encourages each person to openly seek out a solution to the problem. You can eliminate much of the tension that might be present just by creating an atmosphere free from criticism. You can accomplish this by refusing to let any member be attacked by any other member. A simple statement to the effect that "we are not here to criticize each other or hash over the past" will often be all that is necessary.

You can fill each person's need for understanding and acceptance by offering praise and sympathy where warranted. This also builds trust and confidence and further develops the leverage you need to institute the solution. This trust will gain cooperation and attention to your point of view. You will be able to direct the group's efforts toward a rational solution to the problem.

During this interaction, accept each person's comments without making any judgement of his position. Do not accuse him of being in any way to blame for the problem. You may have to listen to emotional statements, bad feelings about others as well as complaints and bitterness about the system. Remember, those feelings are quite normal for a person who is emotionally upset. You need only address your sympathy and understanding to the extent that you let him know that you consider it quite normal, even expected, under conditions of stress.

When dealing with a person that you have determined earlier to be expressing a need for recognition or status, you can provide this status and recognition by your manner of speech. When expressing your point of view, or when referring to the point of view expressed by someone else involved in the conflict, express it as a thought or an opinion. Your purpose is to avoid getting tied down in dogmatic "truth" or "fact." If you talk in terms of thoughts, opinions, feelings and beliefs, soon the other people will be doing the same. Again you are using the leverage of your position to guide the direction of the discussion. Feelings and opinions are much easier to change than are facts or dogma.

Expressing your thoughts in terms of opinions or feelings also removes these statements from the area of conflict. If you say something is your opinion, it would seem rather difficult for someone to argue about it. Anyone can express an opinion without causing someone else to be wrong. Everyone has the right to an opinion and most people will accept that premise.

By showing respect for each person's opinion, your associates learn to show respect for each other's opinion. You may have to point out clearly and strongly that opinions, not hard facts, are being discussed. Often people who are stereotyped in their thinking do not hear the words, opinions or thoughts of others. If you can bring their attention to the fact that everyone else is expressing opinions they will become more aware of their own approach and slowly change to prefacing their own remarks with "I think" or "In my opinion." When this transition takes place, you have won the "war" and only the smaller "clean up" battles are left to sort into place.

How to Use the "Psychology of Suggestion"

Experiments have shown that people do not clearly hear and understand points of view with which they disagree. The portion they do hear is forgotten very quickly. For this reason, it is not very productive to attempt to change a person's views by attacking one point at a time, hoping to win him over with logic. You can change views, however, and one way is through the power of suggestion. You suggest a solution or an idea, one at a time, when the other person is ready or willing to listen. You then allow time for the idea to incubate. This might take an hour or it might take a day. In order to insure success with the suggestion, tie the suggestion into some area of the other person's needs. You can do this by appealing to his job and psychological needs.

By reorienting each person to the real problem, after developing a trusting atmosphere, after satisfying some of his psychological needs, and after developing an atmosphere of sharing opinions rather than one of arguing over facts, you can offer suggestions with a high chance of having them accepted. It is important to make sure the suggestions do not create restrictions or obstacles to either person, so that new conflict will be avoided.

When reorienting someone to the real problem, keep away from areas that are outside of his psychological needs. Probe each person for solutions to the problem. Usually they know the real solutions, but may have them entangled in the conflict so deeply that they don't express them. When a possible solution is suggested, respond to it. Summarize what was said and then tie in your suggestion. You might say, "As I see it there are a number of ways to do this. One is the idea you just expressed. Another is to keep an emergency stock on hand. I would like for you to think about both ideas. Why don't you take some time and think of any problems you might see with both ideas and let me know what you think."

When the other person thinks through the problems of both ideas he will begin to accept your suggestion because as he uses his own logic he integrates the idea into his own thinking. Make sure the suggestion is vivid enough that he understands what you mean. You can determine this by asking him to summarize back to you the two ideas he is going to work on.

If possible, find an overriding area that will provide a common ground for all the individuals involved in the conflict. If each person can be directed to an overriding problem or goal, then this part of the background will be the same for all. From this similar perception of the overriding goal, a solution will be easily found. This objective can be attacked in an objective manner as opposed to becoming involved in personal feelings.

Use Psychological Principles to Establish a Solution

In this fifth step, you move toward the solution or accomplishment of the superordinate goal. You do not try to find the cause of the conflict. Nothing can be accomplished if you wind up placing blame on one particular individual for causing the conflict. You place the problem in the perspective of the larger superordinate goal. Now you want a solution within that common framework.

A very broad definition of the goal will leave room for divergent paths to reach that goal without causing conflict between individual participants. You can, within this broad framework, guide the selection of alternatives so that the common cooperative area of solutions falls within a framework that does not interfere with each person's rights in relation to his personal needs. The solution must be written in such a way that these individual needs are preserved.

When you prepare the alternatives, use some of the words of each person involved in the conflict. This will provide a connection for each person which makes acceptance easier. It helps to have as many alternatives as possible evolved from the group, in order to tie in their words. This is relating to the psychology of each person.

Do not try to evaluate the alternative solutions as you develop them. Just get them listed. Once they are listed, check each one and eliminate those that will interfere with any person's psychological needs. Before making a decision, discuss the suggested solutions with each person involved. If you can get individual agreement, then you are assured that in addition to solving the problem, you have resolved the conflict.

If you do have holdouts at this point, confront them directly, by indicating that you see no reason for their resistance. Ask if there is any area they need more information on, or if there is something you haven't made clear. Make it perfectly clear that you will respond to any reasonable objection but that you expect to hear reasons for their resistance.

Finally, call the group together and explain the solution. Present the solution as one that was worked out by the group themselves. They will each recognize the part they played in it. Since it is theirs, they will make it work. Be assertive, persistent and determined that the problem will be solved.

Once the solution has been established, ask each person to commit himself to achieve the goal. Each person should be asked to commit to a specific method or task or approach in the achievement of the goal. This approach is carefully defined to avoid the old conflict that occurred prior to the problem solution.

How a Midwestern Regional V.P. Eliminated Large Losses by Resolving Management Conflicts. A friend, whom I met through a professional society, was recently promoted to regional vice president of a midwestern manufacturing company. During his initial investigation of the facilities under his jurisdiction he found that one manufacturing plant was deeply in the red. This plant had suffered losses for the past two years, but the current losses were running twice the previous ones. He arranged for interviews with the key people involved in the marketing of the products produced at this location.

Prior to the interviews, Fred, the V.P., heard rumors that everyone at the plant was at everyone else's throat. Since Fred was new to the region, it was easy for him to take a neutral position, as a first step, in resolving whatever conflict he might encounter. Fred first interviewed Mac, the product marketing manager. He asked Mac to review the problems that he saw that were causing them to lose money. From this conversation, Fred found out that Mac was being given orders late in the day by the sales manager. Since these orders were generally for slow moving items that were not carried in inventory, many changes in the production line were required to prepare the orders. These changes were very expensive but had to be made in order to fill the late orders. This, as Mac saw it, was their biggest problem.

When Fred felt he understood the work problem well enough, he began to examine Mac's psychological position. (Step two.) He first asked Mac about the importance of accepting the late orders, from his point of view. At first Mac said, "they are important." When Fred followed with a question about the way in which the late orders were handled, Mac then indicated that he didn't believe it was necessary at all. Fred then asked why the late orders were being taken. At this point, Mac indicated that he believed that many orders were being taken in an attempt to get him "off" the job due to an old grudge the sales manager is holding. Fred discussed this incident in order to let Mac ventilate his feeling.

Fred summarized his understanding of Mac's perception of the problem: "As I understand what you are saying, late orders are being taken unnecessarily and you feel this may be an attempt to create problems that will cause you to lose your job. Is that right?" Mac responded, "Yes." Fred now has Mac's views on the work problem and understands Mac's psychological concern for his security. Fred's job, in relation to Mac, is to find a solution that corrects the problem without threatening Mac's job security.

Fred then asked Mac, "What do you see as a way to solve this problem?" Mac replied, "Eliminate all late orders that are not real emergencies." Fred then used the power of his position (step three) to help fulfill Mac's personal needs. He praised Mac's objective approach to the problem, in spite of his personal feelings about the sales manager.

Fred then suggested (step four) an alternative. He presented the alternative in such a way that he tied into Mac's need for job security. Fred said, "Mac, as I see it, we could get pressure off you by stopping late orders or by placing the responsibility for clearing late orders with the sales manager. How would you feel about the sales manager working directly with the operations manager in the case of late orders? You would still prepare the regular schedule." Mac replied that at first thought that seemed reasonable. "Let those two argue over the changes," he concluded.

Notice that Fred did not try to solve the work problem. He was only concerned with the psychological aspects of the problem. He was also gathering information to be used to solve the work problem later.

Fred went through the same procedure with the operations manager and found that the operations manager automatically cancelled any orders for schedule changes that Mac gave to the foreman. The operations manager felt that Mac was trying to circumvent his authority by going directly to the foreman. These changes are lowering the group's productivity. Wilt, the operations manager, felt that he was the only one who had the authority to change a schedule.

Fred next talked to the two foremen, George and Joe. Both men claimed that they were unable to make their production quotas, due to the changes being made each day. In the past, they had made changes because they were trying to help Mac, without telling their boss, Wilt. Now, however, the changes were getting more numerous and they were complaining to Wilt, in order to stop the changes.

Both foremen felt they could go beyond their production quota, if they could avoid having their people stand around doing nothing while the changeover was being made. Probing their statements, Fred found that a changeover at breaktime or dinner time would not affect production.

Fred next talked to the sales manager. The sales manager informed Fred that the product marketing manager, Mac, was not getting the production that he needed to fill his orders. Hank, the sales manager, said that there was some kind of feud going on between Mac and Wilt and it was destroying his business. A number of large sales had been lost and other customers were threatening to stop doing business with the company. The sales manager felt that he should be the one to determine what products were to be produced and the product manager should schedule accordingly. He believed he was not recognized as a member of management.

After this interview, Fred decided their overriding problem was to fill the orders of the large accounts that were being lost due to shortages. Fred checked the records and found that these large accounts were responsible for the recent increase in changeovers. He sent a memorandum, at that time, to all the key people whom he had interviewed and informed them of the severity of the loss of these accounts. He scheduled a meeting to discuss this single most important problem facing the management team and asked that each one prepare recommendations to solve the problem. His intention was to resolve the schedule conflict as a part of the solution to this new superordinate goal (step five).

When the meeting was held, all the participants were informed that a high degree of cooperation was necessary in order to serve the large accounts. Fred summarized the recommendations the various members had made earlier. These also contained his own inputs. He obtained consensus that each member would function as follows: The product manager would establish the regular quantities that were to be produced. He would turn this schedule over to the operations manager, at which point he would have no further responsibility for scheduling. In cases of emergencies where a product had to be produced that required a schedule change, the sales manager would be totally responsible for the change. He would give the change directly to the operations manager and the operations manager would instruct the foremen.

No one but the operations manager would deal with the foremen. The operations manager would also inform the sales manager of any customer that would be shorted any product as a result of the change over. The sales manager would handle the problem of the shortage with the customer. The product manager would not be involved in this customer contact. The sales manager would also head a new management task force to work toward the elimination of all shortages.

From the alternatives suggested at the meeting, it was decided that a small inventory of slow moving items, especially those purchased by their large customers, would be carried. It developed during the discussion that the total cost of the items and their inventory-carrying charge for one month was less than the cost of changeovers. Any changeover that had to be made would occur at lunch break, and the line would not be changed back until the next break. Any excess production from the changeover, over what was required to fill the current order, would become small order inventory.

Although these solutions seemed simple in retrospect, they were successful because Fred removed the elements that frustrated the psychological needs of each individual. The sales manager was given direct management responsibility, which made him feel part of the management team. The operations manager had his authority restored. The foremen were able to make their production quotas, which satisfied their work-related needs. As a consequence of the cooperative attitude that developed, both foremen shortly thereafter made improvements that increased their productivity.

With the conflict removed, the sales manager and product manager "teamed up" and visited the accounts they had previously lost and were successful in getting most of the business back. The plant started showing a profit and this led to additional enthusiasm which led to further improvement and more profits. The organization now works as a team and the team makes money.

How to Use the Power of Words to Develop Psychological Leverage

The words you use and the way you use them are the main determinants of the impression you make on people. People form a mental image of who and what you are based upon your appearance and your use of words. You can make a good first and lasting impression by utilizing the concepts covered in this chapter.

In this chapter you'll see how to use words to create an image of a clear thinking, intelligent person. By selecting and properly arranging the words you use, you will show people that you have the capacity to think and express yourself clearly. This dynamic impression will give you Psychological Leverage. You will be able to use this leverage to secure more responsible assignments and increased authority.

You can improve the power of your speech by following the guidelines in this chapter. By using the proper words, you can provide people with visualization of the ideas you wish to express. You will see how to gain understanding, become more convincing and gain commitment to your point of view by relating to the psychology of the other person. This approach will give you Psychological Leverage in dealing with all types of people and you will gain recognition and respect for what you say.

FIVE WAYS TO ADD POWER TO YOUR POINT OF VIEW

You can develop the power to influence other people by using a five point system that insures interest receptivity, clarity, understanding and conviction. Each point of the five is related to a specific psychological need of the other person. By appealing to a person's specific need, you gain the leverage of having that person utilize your ideas to fulfill his needs. Your idea is accepted because it becomes a tool that the other person uses to attain his own goals. The five points are:

1. How To Develop A Friendly Atmosphere
2. How To Make Your Message Memorable
3. How To Insure Understanding
4. How To Get Other People Interested In Your Idea
5. How To Keep The Discussion On The Track

How to Develop a Friendly Atmosphere

Educators say a student's learning is dependent upon his readiness to learn. The same principle applies to understanding. If a person is ready to listen, he is more likely to understand. One way to develop this readiness to listen is by developing a friendly atmosphere. If the individual feels you are being friendly as opposed to being critical, he has no reason to block out what you say.

Generally, we are not aware of the impact our words have on people. When you tell others "you're wrong," "you shouldn't," "you should," or use similar phrases that begin with "you," the other person may get the impression you are criticizing him. These "you" oriented words often make the other person feel guilty or "put down." In other words, they create an unfriendly atmosphere.

Often people create an unfriendly atmosphere by taking exception to what some other person says. If you argue or say the other person is wrong, you force him to take a protective stand. In his effort to protect himself, he may become more firmly committed to his position. This position may be biased and reflect the prejudices upon which the original statement was based.

As he argues to protect himself, his thoughts become stereotyped, he closes his mind to rational evidence and directs all his energy toward proving himself right or proving you wrong. Since your criticism of his original statement evoked unfriendly feelings, he is much more likely to take latitude in proving you wrong. If you say his idea won't work, for example, he may lie and say that it has already worked. In this unfriendly atmosphere, you are not likely to get your point of view accepted.

No matter how long the argument goes on, you will not be able to get him to open his mind. As a matter of fact, the longer you argue, the less chance you have of getting him to listen. Why? Because you are asking him to say he was wrong. You are asking him to contradict his original statement.

You can avoid this situation by developing and maintaining a friendly atmosphere. The way to avoid arguments is to avoid stereotyped or "cut and dried" statements. The other person's self-esteem need not be threatened when you disagree with him. To avoid threatening or criticizing, state your arguments in terms of thoughts, opinions and feelings. *Always state your beliefs as being your ideas, thoughts or opinions rather than as being unchallengeable laws.*

If you use terms like "I think," "I feel," "In my opinion," or "I believe," you do not put the other person in a position of having to attack to disagree with you. Also the system is "catching." Soon the other person will begin to use the same phrases. This method of discussion is conducive to a friendly atmosphere, to listening and to understanding.

I have a friend who always opens review sessions with his subordinates by complimenting them on some exceptional effort or accomplishment. Even in cases where they have made major blunders or have not properly performed their duties, he still finds something that they have done well to compliment them on.

He does this to establish a friendly atmosphere. He shows the subordinate, through this initial compliment, that his purpose is to help him overcome his problems, not to criticize him as a person. The compliment shows that he recognizes the subordinate's strengths as well as his weaknesses. This friendly approach encourages the subordinate to try to understand his superior's point of view rather than close his mind by defending himself against attack. This manager's subordinates listen, learn and mature rapidly.

How to Make Your Message Memorable

You can make sure that people remember your message longer by describing your ideas with word pictures. People think in pictures. We visualize pictures when words clearly describe a scene we have seen before. You can test the effectiveness of your message content by visualizing the image your words describe. If you have trouble forming a clear picture from the words you use, the chances are the other person will have even more trouble. You can increase your power of persuasion by visualizing as you speak.

One way to improve the images you describe is to describe your ideas in action. We picture actions more easily than ideas. We easily picture actions that we have been repeatedly exposed to. Such words as run, walk, talk, are easily pictured. You can increase your persuasive effectiveness by using these action words.

For example, if you wish to describe the adversity man faces in life, you can express the idea so that it can be visualized by using an "action" example. You might say, "A man running uphill on a sand dune that gives way under each step he takes, allowing him to move forward only an inch at a time, is typical of the adversity that man faces in the early years of his life." By bringing action into the idea, you give people something they can visualize and remember.

You can gain further effectiveness by using familiar scenes in your descriptions. The more familiar the words, the more easily we visualize them. Tree, house, car, flower, are easily visualized. Of course each word needs more detail if you are describing a specific one as opposed to using the word to help get a general idea across.

We can more easily visualize a specific object or action than a general one. We visualize a red rose more easily than a flower. You can use these "image making" words to improve understanding. If you wish to indicate movement in your idea, you might simply use the word "run" or "running." If you wish to indicate strength, you might refer to a "stone house." If you need a more specific picture for comparison than "the fragrance of a flower," you might say, "the fragrance of a freshly opened yellow rose." You, of course, select the more general or more specific phrase depending upon your purpose.

You can be more effective by using concrete rather than abstract words. People can more easily visualize things than ideas. They can more easily picture a "box" than a cubic area. In those cases where you have to use abstractions, try to find examples that are concrete. If you can relate to a concrete example, you can more easily generate the picture you wish the other person to see.

The abstract idea that inflation is a hidden regressive tax can be more effectively described with concrete examples. One way to do this would be to compare the shrinkage of the value of a rich man's wealth with that of a poor man's wealth. You might say, "The rich man learns to live with his bank account, losing six per cent of its value. The poor man learns to live with six per cent less food and clothing."

People also picture specific things more easily than generalizations. If you tell a person to do something about his departmental expenses, he may not understand that an expense reduction is required. On the other hand, if you tell him to reduce his departmental expenses by ten per cent, he knows exactly what you want. You can improve your results by using specific concrete words in directing the activities of your subordinates. If you want sales increased, tell your subordinates how much you want them improved, how soon you expect to see some results and the product lines or profits you want priority given to.

You can make your ideas more memorable by using active words. Active words are much easier to understand than passive ones. You can formulate the same message with "I" and "We" that you can with "It." The active voice always develops interest. People visualize happenings and the active voice tells who or what is happening. People better understand messages that they can visualize and they can visualize action better than they visualize still scenes.

You can improve your effectiveness even more by using people in your examples. People visualize people more easily than anything else, so any time you can tie the action into people you enhance your chances of getting others to understand you. For example, see how quickly you visualize this scene: The policeman yelled at the small boy running across the intersection against the red light.

How to Insure Understanding

You can generally get better understanding by *speaking in positive terms*. It is just as easy to say, "Walk around the edge," as to say "Avoid the water." People are psychologically motivated to do things to achieve goals. They are attracted to and interested in positive things. But, most people are reminded of their fears by negative suggestions. Since they prefer not to think of their fears, they tend to shut out fear-producing negative thoughts and suggestions.

Another psychological barrier to understanding is distrust. People generally close out and do not try to understand those whom they distrust. Many people distrust anyone who uses big words or long complicated sentences. You can gain trust and understanding by *using simple words and phrases*. It is more trustworthy to say, "Our sales are lower than last year," than to say, "We have experienced a splenetic reaction to our attempts at achieving our sales objectives."

A clear and concise statement won't make the other person accept your point of view but at least he will be able to understand it. And understanding is necessary for acceptance. To be clear, use short, simple, everyday words. Many people know the meaning of "prevaricator" but everyone knows the meaning of "liar."

To be concise, you *keep the sentence short*. One idea coupled with one descriptive phrase is a good guideline. People cannot absorb a long sentence complicated with numerous adjectives and adverbs.

If three or four descriptive phrases are needed to complete an explanation, convert them into separate sentences. Most people won't take the time to unravel a long complicated sentence.

Finally, people need a signal when you are about to change to a new topic. They may lose the train of thought if the transition is not made clear because they are still integrating and thinking about the last point you made. If you don't make a connection for them, you may lose their attention.

You can hold their attention and keep them on your track by using connecting words that show you are changing the subject or moving to a new point. You can use these *transitional words* and phrases to keep people tuned in to what you are saying. By the use of transitions you give them clues to shift their minds from one point to the next. Some examples of transition words are: since, therefore, consequently, however and sometimes. When these simple words that show a shift to a new topic are forgotten, the other person loses continuity and you lose the opportunity for understanding.

How to Get Other People Interested in Your Idea

In your discussion, support your points by example. Since people are interested in other people and events, you can build your examples around people and events to hold their interest. Using examples of people and events not only creates interest but also helps people remember. A good human interest story with a "point" or "moral" will be remembered for a long time. Religious philosophers have been using this system with "parables" for centuries.

People are also interested in new knowledge. If you can present your point of view in such a way that you give new knowledge or skills to the listener, he will show more interest and be more likely to accept your ideas.

Another way to get people interested in your ideas is to find an area of usefulness for the idea. Often an idea is useful in some way that people fail to see. If you can find an area of usefulness and remind them of the use, they generally accept your idea. In this way you help other people and at the same time increase the power of what you say.

You can also use suspense to develop interest in your point of view. People are psychologically attracted to suspense. If you can develop some suspense by revealing your information in steps, people will become interested in your idea. By building from a point of initial interest to a point by point unveiling of your conclusion, you also give them time to absorb and integrate each point into their own mental framework.

Another way to get people interested in your ideas is to relate your idea as "hot news." People are attracted to hot news. New products, product improvements, personnel changes or policy changes are examples from business that could be utilized as hot news.

How to Keep the Discussion on the Track

You can keep people from wandering away from the subject you wish to discuss. People who wander from the topic you are discussing are reacting to their internal motivational drives and are difficult to converse with. They can be kept on the track, however, by using statements related to the original topic, or by probing.

When a person whom you are talking to wanders off the subject, bring his attention back by a probe such as, "Do you see any problem with the change we've been talking about?" By asking a question, you relate to his psychological need for freedom to speak. At the same time you are exercising Psychological Leverage, by bringing him back to the topic you want to discuss.

The following techniques will help keep people on the track:

1. Clearly state your purpose, intent or procedure to be discussed.
2. Indicate the consequences or results expected from your proposal.
3. Provide illustrations, comparisons and examples.
4. Speak at a rapid pace.
5. Clearly state your evidence and conclusion.

All of the techniques presented in this chapter are important in keeping the other person on the track. You need to gain attention and interest and state your message clearly and concisely. Keep a rapid pace, present only one idea at a time and probe for understanding. Make sure you keep a friendly atmosphere, speak in non-critical terms and state your points as ideas, thoughts, beliefs or opinions. By using these ideas you will be able to keep the discussion on the track which will improve your effectiveness in making your point

A Pep-Talk That Increased Productivity. The operations manager of a mid-western packaging plant called a meeting of all his production foremen. He opened the meeting by commenting on a specific area that each foreman had excelled in. He pointed out that similar results in their other duties would substantially lower their production cost.

He related those productivity increases to actual dollar bonuses the foremen would earn at the end of each semi-annual reporting period. He described a winter vacation with one foreman skiing down a snow covered mountain. He pictured another on the ocean cruise he was always talking about. He pointed out specific results that would be required to earn the bonuses that would enable each man to fulfill some need that each had expressed an interest in.

The operations manager asked for ideas from each foreman and asked them to give each other ideas on how to accomplish their goals. He promised to keep them informed on their progress and did so each week. By the end of the sixth week all departments were running at a level that would meet the new goals. Each foreman earned his bonus at the end of the period.

THREE KEYS IN USING THE PSYCHOLOGY OF THE OTHER PERSON TO DOUBLE YOUR WORD POWER

The secret of relating to the psychology of the other person is to recognize the differences in the way each person perceives the world around him. If you are aware of the large number of different possibilities, you can add the specific details that are necessary to relate what you say to the psychology of each person.

There are three basic keys that will help you double the power of what you say, by relating to the psychology of the other person. The three keys are:

1. Using Words That Evoke Mental Images
2. Speaking For The Ear Of The Beholder
3. Adjusting To The "Listening Absorption" Rate

1. Using Words That Evoke Mental Images

Recent research has shown that over eighty per cent of what people learn, they learn visually. You can double even triple the understanding you get from people if you can relate what you say to the psychology of the other person and evoke pictures in his mind that are consistent with your intended meaning.

People form mental pictures for words they hear, but each person forms a different picture. The word "chair" for example may evoke a number of different pictures. One person may visualize a stuffed chair, another may see a wooden chair and perhaps another person may picture a rocking chair. Which one did you picture?

People form various mental images, or meanings, based upon

their own personal motivations, experiences and background. People who are contemplating the purchase of a rocking chair will form that image. People who are contemplating relaxing in a stuffed chair will think of a stuffed chair and so on. Each individual will imagine a picture consistent with his own psychological motivation.

People need illustrations and examples that clearly illustrate your meaning. Human interest stories may be used to accomplish this purpose. You can emphasize important points by dramatization and by relating an "action" example that clearly illustrates your point. To explain "using double your usual power," for example, you might say, "I'm as powerful as a double-barreled shot gun, cocked and ready. And I'm going to fire both barrels at once."

2. Speaking for the Ear of the Beholder

The person you are speaking to may hear your words but may not hear your meaning. Words are generalizations and the other person hears them from his own perceptual framework. The real meaning of a word is in the mind of the "beholder," the listener. If you can relate to this psychology of the other person, you can more easily get your ideas accepted.

The ear of the beholder is a receptor that is finely tuned to each individual's personal psychology. Each individual tunes his ear in to messages that relate to his motivations and tunes out those that are irrelevant. You can improve the power of what you say by keeping your words relevant to the other's personal motivations.

One way to relate to the motivations of the other person is to use some of his words. You can use his words or favorite phrases to place emphasis on key points you are trying to make. You relate to his total need system by using his expressions. The more of his words and phrases that you use, the more closely your meaning will match his perceptions.

Suppose, for example, that you want a new drill press to be used in a machine shop. Further assume that you know the operator uses words like "top flight" and "cream of the crop." You can use those words when describing the drill press. You might say "This is a top flight machine. Try it out, this drill bit is the cream of the crop."

You can also improve understanding by using colorful examples. People are attracted to colorful phrases that make an explicit point. For example, to describe a smoothly running organization, you might say, "The organization runs as smoothly as a well oiled motor." When using colorful examples, stick with familiar descriptions. Most people know the sound of a jet engine but many would not know the sound of an old "Tin Lizzie."

The ear of the beholder is impatient and wants to get on with the relevant facts and figures. Use as few words as you can, that still express what you want to say. The number of words you use in expressing your opinion is a direct example of your mental ability. Those who listen to you can tell quickly whether or not you are a well organized person. The organization of your sentences, in speech, reflects how well you understand your topic. If you spend five minutes explaining what could be covered in one sentence, you will give the impression that you really haven't thought out what you are saying. With a little forethought, you can narrow your words down to short simple sentences that clearly explain your point of view.

The ear of the beholder prefers suggestions to orders. People resent being told what to do, so they build defenses against orders. From early childhood people are pounded with what to do and when to do it. So make suggestions, rather than give orders. Suggestions are more pleasing to the ear. They work most of the time.

The ear of the beholder is attracted to action. So use action words. Since many different words may be used to express the same thought, you have a choice in selecting the words to express any thought. To get action into your message use movement in your descriptions. Instead of saying, "There is a man on the corner," say, "The man is pacing on the corner" or "moving toward the corner." Action holds attention which promotes understanding.

3. Adjusting to the "Listening Absorption" Rate

The time you spend on any one idea will have a direct influence on how much attention the listener gives you. You must adjust your pace to fit the absorption rate of your listeners. Again, you relate to the psychology of the other person by speaking at a pace that will be comfortable for him. If you spend too much time on one idea, your listener will become bored and tune out. So it is usually better to develop a fast pace than a slow one.

In order to keep your listener "tuned in" spend just enough time to adequately cover your idea. State it clearly and concisely, provide only enough detail to insure understanding and then move to your next point.

When discussing a new topic, express only one idea at a time. No one can hold more than one picture in his mind at one time. Each person also needs time to integrate each idea into his thinking. If you move to a new topic too quickly, the first image will be lost and your idea will not be evaluated. Give the other person time to evaluate and absorb each idea before moving to the next one. If you can get him to think about it in relation to something he is familiar with, he will more quickly absorb the idea. This can be accomplished with suggestions and questions for understanding. This is the only way you can be sure you have understanding.

The "Doublespeak" Award

The National Council of Teachers of English recently awarded the State Department the "Doublespeak" award. The State Department won the award with the most complex "gobbledygook" of the year. Rather than trying to write clear, concise, understandable English, the State Department came out with this award winner: "The coordinator will review existing mechanisms of consumer input, throughput and output and seek ways of improving these linkages via the consumer communication channel."

It is clear that very few people would understand what the coordinator is supposed to do. Unless the coordinator has additional information, I doubt that he himself knows what to do.

One way to stop those people who use unduly complex sentences is to ask them to define each word they use that you don't understand. It's amazing how these people can find simple phrases to explain their complex words and sentences. You wonder why they didn't use the simple explanations when they first spoke.

How a Sales Manager Used Word Power to Solve a Sales Problem. Larry, a sales manager of a West Coast bottling company, received an order for a truckload of "twelve-packs" from a new customer. The order had to be shipped the next day or it would not be accepted. Larry found that only "six-packs" were being produced and there was no inventory of "twelve-packs." Knowing that changeovers from "six-packs" to "twelve-packs" were expensive, Larry knew he would have to be very persuasive to get the change made.

Larry went into the office of Earl, the operations manager. Earl was on the phone arguing with someone. Larry could see that his timing was wrong; Earl was not in a state of readiness for listening. In order to gain Psychological Leverage, Larry became a sounding board for Earl's problems. He listened patiently, expressed understanding and encouraged Earl to "talk it out." Larry developed a friendly atmosphere and earned an obligation from Earl to listen to him.

When Earl had gotten his irritations talked out, he was ready and willing to listen to Larry. Larry carefully formulated words that pictured the loss of his orders as "the first brick falling from a crumbling building." Then he used active and positive words to stress the necessity for building strong ties with his customer, ties that would withstand the depressing cycles of their seasonal business. This customer, Larry explained, would be a consistent year round customer.

Larry explained that there would be problems from time to time, but that over a period of a year, the account would more than pay for the occasional problems. Earl "tuned in" to the word problem. He began to talk about plant problems again. Larry brought him back on the track. He told Earl that he had a problem getting the new account started and needed his cooperation in filling the first order.

Earl asked what the problem was and Larry explained. Earl resisted making the production change but said he understood Larry's problem. Larry again listened to Earl's reason for resisting and then repeated his expectations for large future orders based upon successfully handling the current order in line with the customer's conditions.

Larry had built Psychological Leverage with the power of his words. Earl finally agreed to make the production change. Larry's order was filled and the company benefitted from a continuing flow of business from the new customer.

7

How to Use the Linking Technique to Motivate People

You can gain commitment from people by linking the rewards of task accomplishment to the satisfaction of their psychological needs. When people see that certain actions will fulfill or satisfy their needs, they become motivated to perform that action. They then become more interested in and are committed to the diligent completion of the task, whatever it might be.

In this chapter you will be introduced to specific techniques that utilize each individual's motivational drives to get what you want done. You'll see how this Psychological Leverage will help get your point of view accepted and acted upon. You will also learn to distinguish between the basic human needs and see how to appeal to each of them in such a way that you gain each person's commitment.

By recognizing the basic needs that we all have, you can relate to those needs to get people to be more productive. You'll learn three ways, in this chapter, to determine the needs that motivate each individual. Once you learn the predominant need that is motivating any person, you will be able to relate to that need in two different ways, either of which will give you the Psychological Leverage needed to accomplish your goal.

HOW MOTIVATION RELATES TO NEEDS AND GOALS

People strive to achieve certain "satisfiers" such as water, food, rest and relaxation to fulfill their biological need to stay alive. We also strive for other "satisfiers" such as friendship, freedom and perhaps a "pat on the back" to fulfill our psychological needs for sociability, self-realization and esteem. If our supply of food, or any of the other "satisfiers" of our biological needs is cut off, we become tense. The same tension develops when we are deprived of the "satisfiers" of our psychological needs.

This internal tension motivates us to action and directs our action toward a goal. The goal is the achievement of the "satisfier" that we were lacking or were deprived of. So, we can define motivation in terms of needs and goals. *Motivation is a drive resulting from an internal tension to achieve a goal determined by our individual expectations which will generate an action utilizing learned behavior that does not conflict with our individual value system.*

BASIC MOTIVATORS: THE KEY TO GETTING YOUR POINT ACROSS

Motivation is the key to getting your point of view accepted. Since each person is motivated by different needs and expectations, you can more easily get your point across if you can determine the need that is motivating a person. The need or expectation that is motivating an individual at a particular time will direct the interest and attention of that person. If you wish to get your view accepted, you must give consideration to tying your idea into the motivation of the person you are talking to.

The most basic and most easily understood of all the research and theory proposed on motivation is the work done by Dr. Abraham Maslow (1954). His studies show that man progresses from a lower to a higher level of needs. As the lower level biological needs (air, water, food, etc.) are fulfilled, man progresses to the next higher level, the security needs (safety, job security, emotional security, etc.) and then to the next level, the social needs (friendship and love) and then to the next level, esteem needs (status, power, recognition) and finally, self-actualization needs (growth, challenge, change).

The self-actualization level is never fulfilled. We may reach self-actualization by reaching our potential or by satiating our interest in one project, but then there are always new ones to capture our imagination. As we read a book on a new subject, for example, we learn of something we are not familiar with. This new knowledge triggers a desire to learn more about the new subject. So we may search out new books or actual experiences to develop our potential in the new subject area.

So we never reach a level where all our needs are fulfilled. As each need is fulfilled a new one pops up to take its place. Also, old needs that were previously fulfilled continue to pop back up. If we are not in contact with other people for a period of time, our social needs pop up again. Any need, even though it was previously fulfilled, comes back into prominence when we are deprived of the experiences that satisfy those needs. We generally follow patterns of behavior each day that substantially fill all our needs.

We should really not say that any need is ever completely fulfilled. It would be more realistic to say that a need is substantially fulfilled. Even though our bank account may grow to a balance large enough to provide for our comforts for the rest of our lives, we would still have some concern for security. We could say, however, that our security needs were substantially fulfilled.

HOW THE "LINKING TECHNIQUE" RELATES TO MOTIVATION: THE SECRET OF GETTING THINGS DONE

So we see that all of us are really motivated to a larger or lesser degree by all the basic needs listed by Dr. Maslow. We are all to some extent motivated by biological security, social esteem and self-actualization needs.

These needs vary in intensity, depending upon their importance to each of us. If I have been deprived of water for a few hours, my biological need for water will start to intensify. The longer I go without water the more intense the need will become. Soon every mental and physical action that I take will be directed toward getting water. All other thoughts and awareness will be driven from my mind. I will be consciously and unconsciously driven to find water.

This internal drive to fulfill the need for water is also an example of how we are internally driven to fulfill our psychological needs. So we say that motivation is internally developed. You can influence people by tying in to that internal motivation. You can develop Psychological Leverage by linking your ideas to the needs of the other person. If your attempt to influence is inconsistent with the other person's motivation, you will not be effective in your efforts to persuade him.

Here then is the secret of getting your point of view accepted, the secret of motivating people. You simply find a part of your idea or a part of the job that is an ingredient in the fulfillment of the other person's needs. You can then tie in your persuasive efforts to helping the other person fulfill those needs. If you can determine the individual's motivating need and link your ideas or job assignments to that need, the individual will be internally motivated to achieve the goals or accept the ideas you propose.[1]

A Federal Attempt at Minority Job Training. During the 1960's, the federal government funded job training programs for minorities. The idea was to provide job skills to the hard-core unemployed. Training programs were set up in major cities throughout the United States and trainers were brought in to do the job.

One of the objectives developed by the training staff was to help the trainees learn enough to feel proud of their new skills. In presenting their material, the instructors constantly related to the pride, sense of accomplishment and recognition the trainees would be able to gain from the program.

The overall program was a failure. The trainees did not respond to the motivational efforts of the instructors. Many of the trainees dropped out of the program without apparent cause. Many dropped out due to pressure from the instructors, etc. Very few completed the program.

A later research study uncovered many of the reasons for the failure. One of the major reasons the program failed was related to the trainee's psychological needs. The instructors related their material to the wrong needs. The trainees were motivated by security needs, not by esteem needs that the instructors were relating to. The trainees wanted to learn how to get a job and how to keep it. Their primary motivation, and consequently the one relationship they would have responded to, was how the job skills would insure them of receiving a check each week on a permanent basis.

Solving Family Problems. I have found that solving family problems is no more difficult than business problems. The same techniques that are used to help adult members of organizations can be used to help children. The Linking Technique can be used to get your point across to children.

I have found that children frequently leave a family discussion with a completely different understanding than the one intended by the parent.

I overcame this problem by relating my ideas in terms that help the child see the relationship between the idea and his own needs.

For example, I was able to instill a strong aversion to smoking in the minds of my children by relating to their desire to be independent.

By pointing out throughout their childhood that smoking usually started because of group pressure to conform to group standards, I was able to prepare them to exert their independence. Two of my three adult children have never smoked. The third began smoking only after he had attained adulthood. They clearly understood that smoking would be conforming to the will of others which would be a loss of their own independence.

HOW TO DETERMINE PEOPLE'S NEEDS
THROUGH DISCUSSION

You can influence people by linking the benefits that may be derived from completing a task or performing a task in the work situation to the individual's psychological needs. If you show an individual that the completion of a task will provide some of the satisfaction he is seeking, he will become more productive.

In order to provide this satisfaction, you must first determine the specific needs that motivate this person. Once you are aware of these needs, you can help him fulfill them by linking a task-related benefit to that need. He will then be internally motivated to accomplish the task leading to that benefit. The following techniques will help determine an individual's needs.

The same tensions that motivate people to act to seek satisfaction for a need motivate them to talk about their needs and goals. If you have talked with a particular person in the past, he probably revealed many of his needs during the conversation. You can think back to the conversation and, by analyzing the things he talked about, determine some of his needs.

Using Problems to Uncover Needs

You can get people to talk about their needs if you are friendly. If you express friendliness, they will feel comfortable in talking to you and reveal many of their needs through conversation.

Ask easy questions to get people talking. You might ask, "How do you like it here?" or "What problems do you have here?" Often a person will talk about problems that he sees on the job when he won't talk directly about his own needs. The problem-oriented discussion will reveal his own personal interest which is a reflection of his needs. Another question such as, "How do you think we could improve things here?" may provide answers that reflect his needs.

Gaining Information Through Group Discussion

You can gain more information, usually, from group discussion than from a one-on-one discussion. People who are reluctant to speak openly to a superior, often gain courage from their peers in group meetings. You can encourage their participation by first getting their peers to talk. After hearing their fellow team members speak out, the more reluctant members begin to speak also.

During these discussions, all members tend to express their own needs and goals. By listening and questioning you will be able to determine their needs. You might ask questions such as, "How will this change affect you?" or "What problems do you think this change will cause?" Their answers will reflect their individual needs.

Linking Benefits to Needs

During a discussion, suppose one person speaks of trying new things, of making experiments and of seeking new achievements. You can relate those statements to Maslow's model of basic human needs and determine the motivating drive for that person.[2]

Seeking new things and new achievements falls into the self-actualization category. You then know that this person has a need to fulfill, to satisfy his motivation for self-actualization. You can then use the Linking Technique to relate anything new, experimental or challenging about your idea to this individual. The easiest way to persuade is to find a benefit to satisfy the needs the other person is already motivated to fulfill. In this person's mind, challenges and trying new things and achievements are those benefits.

Suppose the other person's needs are for esteem. A person with esteem needs is motivated to seek expressions of praise or recognition from other people. In his conversations he will make statements that describe his power, independence, wisdom, ability and accomplishments. To get your idea across to this person, you must let the idea become his. You can question what he thinks about each point until he accepts the idea as his own. If the idea will enhance his status, prestige, recognition or power, you can help him fulfill his need and at the same time, by using the Linking Technique, motivate higher performance.

People who are primarily motivated by social needs also talk about their needs. They speak of the joy of friendship or their desire to spend more time with people. Since they like people, they have a tendency to describe everyone in glowing terms. They see the best in people and make excuses for their shortcomings. People who are primarily motivated by social needs, need to talk. They talk continually about social, sports or other events. One of the clues that they are socially motivated is that they talk too much. Again, if you can relate your idea in terms that provide a satisfaction of this person's social needs, he will be more likely to accept the idea. If he can see the social relationship in the idea or job assignment, he will tend to commit himself to the job or idea.

The person who is primarily motivated by security needs will express fear of any situation that is not familiar to him. If he has not had experience with an idea or situation, he will fear that its consequences will affect him adversely. In his mind the best thing to do is to stick with the familiar. The familiar, he can trust. The best way to get your idea across to a security oriented person is to make it seem familiar to him. Take each part of the idea and link it to something he is already familiar with.

Personal trust is very important in dealing with the security oriented person. If he has extremely high trust in you, he will also trust your ideas if they are presented in a non-threatening way. Since all people have some of all of the needs at one time or another, be prepared for any of them to emerge at any time. Be prepared for every person to express some need for security at some time.

THE PSYCHOLOGY OF INCORRECT ASSUMPTIONS

You can learn the needs of the most secretive person by using this technique. People who tend to withhold information are usually motivated by some fear. This same fear will work in your favor, if you present this person with an assumption that turns out to be incorrect. Because this person will fear some undue consequence of your incorrect assumption, he will correct your statement.

You can develop statements intended to make this person aware of some problem or adverse consequence for a particular action or situation. Then present your assumption as though you thought this person were involved in the situation. He will very quickly clear up your incorrect assumption. Also, he will usually continue giving you information to make sure you clearly see that he is not involved. This additional information gives you the understanding that you may not otherwise be able to obtain from a secretive person.

I have found incorrect statements to be very effective in dealing with secretive people. When you incorrectly state some assumed association between them and some group activity, they quickly open up. Since secretive people generally do not get involved in group activities, they are quick to clear up the misunderstanding. The incorrect assumption generates a mild internal fear, which the individual will try to alleviate by correcting your assumption.

Once this person explains that he is not or was not involved in the situation you described, you can question for additional information about his needs and goals. At this point he will be anxious to set the record straight. Since you held one incorrect assumption, he may be strongly concerned that you hold others. He will provide the information you want in order to keep you from forming other incorrect assumptions.

Some people want to be recognized as people who are forthright and confident. They want the prestige of feeling they are part of a high status group. They prove this by revealing information, confidentially of course, that came from "inside" circles or confidential sources.

The incorrect assumption can be made about any topic the individual has knowledge of. He will very quickly correct the assumption in order to establish his position as being "in the know."

To determine his real position, you simply relate the assumptions to his goals and needs. He will jump to correct them. This technique, making an incorrect assumption, will increase your knowledge of the other person's needs. You can then increase the power of what you say by linking task-related benefits to this person's needs.

CONTROL TECHNIQUES THAT DETERMINE NEEDS

You can control a conversation by asking the other person for his opinion on topics that you wish to discuss. Often, people will continually wander to other topics. You can always bring them back to the topic of your choice by asking for their opinion.

This technique is extremely effective because, while bringing the other person back to your topic, you allow him freedom of expression. He can fulfill many of his needs through the process of conversation. He can fulfill his need to socialize by speaking about any topic. He can fulfill his need for power through the freedom to speak openly on the topic of your choice. He can express his need for esteem by giving his ideas and opinions, while you listen. You actually help fulfill those needs by listening to him, yet, at the same time, you maintain control.

How People Reveal Their Hidden Motivations

Psychologists tell us that people reveal their motivations as they describe other people and events. A person who tells you that most people are suspicious of others is revealing that he himself is suspicious. If he says most people take advantage of others, it may mean that he takes advantage of others, or wants to. A person who tells you that his associates are dissatisfied probably is revealing his own dissatisfaction.

These revelations occur when people are expressing their views on how other people or groups feel, think or act. The exception, of course, is when they report research findings or have explicit proof for their comments. You can determine the validity of their beliefs by asking how they reached the conclusion. By following the control technique of asking for opinions, you will evoke revelations of each person's needs. Again you are in a position to link task benefits to each person's needs, thereby influencing them to do a better job.

Questions That Reveal People's Needs

Open-end questions that begin by asking "what," "how," "why" or "tell me about" are effective ways to get others to talk enough to tell you their needs. You might say, "What's your opinion?," "How do you think this will work out?" or "Why do you feel that way?" These open-end questions will bring out the other person's feelings, beliefs, thoughts and opinions.

If you wish to tightly control a conversation without eliciting thoughts and opinions from the other person, you may use closed-end questions. These are questions that start with: "when," "where," "can," "will," "is there" and "are there." These closed-end questions require a "yes" or "no" answer or a one word answer. They should be used sparingly as they restrict the other person's freedom and interfere with the fulfillment of his needs.

LINKING INDIVIDUAL AND ORGANIZATIONAL GOALS

When people clearly see that accomplishing organizational goals will help accomplish their own goals, they work diligently toward organizational objectives. I have been constantly amazed to discover that many employees do not see the relationship between their own tasks and the higher goals of the organization. I have found equally surprising the lack of understanding about the relationship between a person's needs and his work goals. As a manager, you must point out this relationship. If you do, you will increasingly find that your subordinates will be more responsive to your directions and will be more productive.

HOW TO DEVELOP THE LINK TO WORK-RELATED GOALS: FIVE KEY TECHNIQUES

People have job-related needs that are just as important as are their personal needs. These job needs grow out of their psychological needs. The desire to do a good job relates to a person's need for competency, to feel that he is capable. By knowing that he is doing a good job, he feels secure in the ability to provide for himself. Most people feel the desire to achieve something and need to achieve their goals for a sense of accomplishment. Psychologists tell us that achievement is one of the most powerful motives that people have.

The Achievement Link

You can influence people by showing the link to the need for achievement. You might say, "Joe, this looks like it is going to be another record for you." This reminder of the high achievement level will link the job performance to Joe's need for achievement. This simple reminder will trigger his subconscious desire to achieve the goal. He will probably now work harder to achieve the goal.

The Competence Link

The same application applies to a person's need to do a job well. All research to date has found that people want to be competent in their work. Again a simple reminder will trigger their desire to fulfill this need. Tied closely to the need to do a job well, is the need to improve performance. Almost everyone wants to improve his performance to satisfy the need for competence or to fulfill the need for self-confidence.

The Salary Link

Salary is another benefit that can be linked to higher performance. People are motivated by salary, despite current opinions to the contrary. Some studies, which may not have covered a sufficient number of variables for so complex a subject, have been interpreted to show that salary is not a motivator. Money, or salary, is a human "satisfier" and is therefore a motivator. It is always a motivator for a majority of the people, but not always for the same reason. People seek money for many different reasons. One person may want it to establish his status, power or freedom. Another may want it for security or to increase his social contacts. Still another may want it strictly to satisfy his standard of living. You can use money as a link between the subordinate's performance and the fulfillment of his needs.

The Feedback Link

People like an organized work system and a way to measure their progress. You can provide feedback on their results which tells them where they stand in relation to their goals. Since they are internally motivated to reach their goals, this feedback will act as a stimulus encouraging them to improve their performance. You can use charts, letters, graphs or verbal systems to provide the information.

The Freedom Link

Many people work best without supervision. They do better if they have some freedom for experimentation. They feel cramped if they have no way to express their diversity. If the job can be structured in such a way that the subordinate has some leeway in the performance of his task, he will again improve his performance in the expression of his needs. Sometimes he will make mistakes, but he will realize it is his mistake and will be motivated to catch up, in order to correct the error. You can link the freedom aspects of a job to his need for independence.

HOW TO DEVELOP THE LINK TO PERSONAL GOALS

Personal goals are people's goals for wealth, property, food, self satisfaction, freedom, independence, etc. They are goals usually not associated with the job, but they derive from the same basic psychological needs that job goals evolve from.

To link job goals to personal needs, again you find a job-benefit that will fulfill one of the personal needs. For example, if you want a subordinate to change to a new job, you pick an element from the job that will appeal to one of his needs.[3]

Perhaps the job is more technical, requiring additional training, is not on a seniority roster and offers more security than other jobs in the same pay range. It is also an important stage in production, which management watches closely.

You pick the linking element that has the most chance of satisfying each person's personal needs. A person who wants a challenge would respond to the highly technical aspect of the job. So you would point out the challenging aspect of learning this highly technical job. The Linking Technique is to clearly state how the technical requirements of the job will satisfy the subordinate's personal needs which he is already motivated to achieve.

When trying to get someone to improve his performance, first dig deep enough to be sure you understand his underlying motivation. Once you are sure that he likes challenges, for example, then you can make the link to that need. You can challenge him to improve rather than criticize mistakes. You can refer to new skills that will lead to greater achievement.

To another who seeks recognition, you can point out the changes that will bring recognition. To those who seek security, find a task that provides security. For the socially motivated, find a job that provides some opportunity for socialization. If you can structure jobs to fit the needs of people you will see their productivity rise.

Remember that people are different. Even though there are overriding group goals that the group aspires to, each person has his own individual goals. These goals differ for each person. Be careful when you use "blanket" statements intended to cover everyone. You may miss them all.

Caution: The Link That Failed. I once knew a salesman who was investing in real estate. He started by buying individual houses, with the intention of building up an equity large enough to trade in for a large apartment complex. As often as he could save enough to buy another house he would do so. He didn't talk a great deal about his investments, but over time I learned of his goals.

I then began to link job benefits to this goal. I would point out that winning a certain sales contest would provide money toward the eventual purchase of the apartment complex. From time to time I would point out a promotion possibility and indicate that the accompanying monetary progress would help him reach his goal.

Eventually I noticed that the salesman was not making any progress. Occasionally he would increase his sales, but after a short time they would drop back to their previous level. Knowing this individual was working toward a specific goal that could be achieved through the rewards of job performance, I could not understand this lack of progress.

I arranged a meeting and asked how he was progressing on his plan to purchase an apartment building. "Oh, I'm not planning on that anymore. I've found something safer," he said. The word "safer" rang through my mind like thunder. I don't know why I had not seen it before. I had wasted two years appealing to the wrong need. I was linking a job benefit to the need for esteem and self-realization and, as it turned out, this salesman was motivated by security needs.

I had failed because I did not do enough "homework." I did not analyze his caution, his reluctance to talk and his resistance to coming into the office. His motivation in buying an apartment was not the challenge to grow or to achieve new things. His motivation was security. He wanted something to provide a living for himself so he wouldn't have to worry about losing his job.

As it turned out, he had been in a position to buy an apartment building twice, but each time backed out due to his fear of failure. I changed my approach and related to his need for security from that time on. I was never able to build him into an outstanding performer because being in the "limelight" would scare him. I was able to help him make progress in small steps, however, that did not scare or worry him.

Footnotes, Chapter 7

[1]V. R. Buzzota, Ph.D., R. E. Lefton, Ph.D., and Manuel Sherberg, Effective Selling Through Psychology: Dimensional Sales and Sales Management Strategies. (New York: Wiley Interscience, 1972), page 288.

[2]*Ibid.*, page 288.

[3]*Ibid.*, page 288.

8

How to Use Psychological Leverage to Get Commitment

When people are committed to an idea or belief, they tend to dedicate themselves to the achievement of goals or objectives that relate to those ideas and beliefs. You can develop Psychological Leverage, which will multiply the power of what you say, by tying in to these underlying motivations of the people you deal with.

In this chapter I'll show you four psychology-based principles which will help you develop this leverage. These principles have been field-tested and proven in everyday business situations. They have also been successfully applied in a wide range of social situations.

These four principles relate to the internal motivations of the other person. You will see how to tie your idea or objective to those internal factors that evoke personal commitment. Then, I'll cover the use of an action plan to crystalize and direct that commitment.

FOUR PSYCHOLOGY-BASED STEPS THAT INSURE COMMITMENT

When an individual is strongly committed to a course of action, he will utilize all his skills and knowledge in performing that action. Because of this commitment, he will look for better techniques and accept changes that lead to higher productivity. This eagerness to improve, results from the motivation to live up to his personal beliefs and principles in fulfilling his goals.

118

Getting Commitment to Job Goals

As a manager, you can use Psychological Leverage to evoke commitment from your subordinates. You can present your job objectives in such a way that you tie in to the subordinate's motivations. You do this by using words that relate the job objectives to the person's personal needs. If the person sees how the job objectives will help him achieve a personal goal, which may simply be a way for him to demonstrate a conviction or belief, he will become committed to the job objective.

In one instance, a brass casting worker objected to the use of a new casting device that was being introduced into the brass foundry where he worked. The new device was so much more efficient than the old one, that the employee feared the loss of overtime that he had previously enjoyed.

During the conversation, the employee explained how he was saving his overtime pay for the "rainy day," when the foundry might shut down and leave him out of work. The "Linking Technique" was used, in this case, to tie in to the subordinate's personal need for security.

One of the major advantages of the new casting device was the time savings which generated a substantial cost reduction in the finished product. This cost reduction would enable the company for the first time to win competitive-bid contracts. Business was expected to double within six months. This would make the company financially secure, and the employees would no longer have to worry about lay-offs. A piece-rate incentive plan was also established to permit the employees to recoup part of the lost overtime wages. When the casting worker saw that his job was more secure and that he would earn extra money on a regular work schedule, he became committed to the new device.

Overcoming Doubts That Affect Commitment

Often people don't utilize their full range of skills due to fear or self-doubt. Dr. Abraham Maslow, in *Motivation and Personality* (Harper and Row, 1954), concluded that many people hold grave doubts about their ability. Many actually fear using their full ability or achieving their potential. They fear the consequences of changes that may take place as a result of greater performance.

You can use Psychological Leverage to help these people by

evoking their commitment to a higher goal. You can weave reinforcing phrases into your discussion that will hold down this person's fear. Phrases such as "It is an easy task," "It won't cause big changes," or "Things will be more stable" will help this person feel safe in pursuing the new objective.

1. HOW TO TIE YOUR IDEAS TO THE OTHER PERSON'S MOTIVATIONS

If you can demonstrate that your idea or opinion will help fulfill one of the other person's needs, without requiring him to abandon his value system or integrity, he will accept the idea. The more closely your ideas mesh with the needs or goals of the other person, the more strongly he will be committed to using your idea or following your instructions. Your Psychological Leverage is in using the other person's need to achieve his previously held goals or objectives in carrying out your instructions.

Developing a "Fit" Between an Idea and a Conviction

People are comfortable with ideas or instructions that mesh with their previously held convictions. Those convictions generally cover a wide range of subjects and can be determined by the previously explained probing techniques.

People generally hold beliefs in "sets" rather than as single convictions. A set of convictions represents a person's attitude about a particular subject. Generalizations are made from this set to cover new or similar situations. You can develop Psychological Leverage by forming a generalization that is a "fit" between your idea or objective and a specific set of convictions held by the other person.

An Example of Using the "Fit" Technique to Change Opinions. A salesman who called on the buyer of a national variety store chain felt helpless to cope with the behavior of the chain buyer. This buyer was courteous and responsive to the salesman's presentation, but never gave an order to the salesman. The Variety Line salesman would work out all the details of a regional or national promotion for the buyer and the buyer would say, "I'll let you know."

A day or two later, the buyer would contact the salesman's boss and complete arrangements for the order. This action left the salesman feeling left out. "The buyer treats me like I'm nothing," he said. "I prepare all the details, do the leg-work, prepare production schedules, arrange shipping details, advertising and promotional support, and then the buyer places the order with my boss."

When the salesman questioned the buyer about bypassing him and giving the order to his boss, the buyer simply stated that he wanted the sales manager's assurance that all details would be properly handled.

A careful analysis of this buyer's remarks, during various discussions, led to the following profile of his convictions. The buyer believed that young people today were not conscientious. "People should stand on their own two feet and make their own way in the world," was his favorite expression. He thought young people should be more responsible in their approach to life and work. At one point he indicated that the Variety Line salesman was a little young for the job.

This problem was resolved by developing an idea that would create a "fit" between the buyer's convictions about young people and the salesman's objective of having the buyer place the order directly with him.

The "fit" was developed to relate to the buyer's conviction that young people should be more responsible. The statement of the "fit" was, *"Young people need the opportunity to take responsibility for handling all the details of a project on their own, so they can develop the ability to stand on their own two feet."* The Variety Line salesman asked to be given full responsibility for the next promotion, including the placement of the order. The buyer, faced with the choice of agreement or the denial of his own convictions, agreed to the request.

2. HOW TO TIE YOUR IDEAS TO THE OTHER PERSON'S SELF-IMAGE

One reason a person may reject an idea or attitude is that he believes that it is not consistent with his self-image. He will more likely accept an attitude, idea or persuasion that is similar to or consistent with his self-image.

If a person holds an image of himself as an aggressive, pushy, self-centered person, he will accept arguments that the rest of the world is the same way. He will accept as "true" arguments that it's a "dog-eat-dog" world. The statement "Everyone is out to get what he can" is interpreted by him to mean "out to take advantage of others." All arguments that portray people as being hostile or selfish will be readily accepted by the person who holds a hostile self-image.

A person who has a hostile self-image will be likely to attribute the kind acts of others to some hidden motive. Since people often have multiple motives for doing things, he can usually find some motive that seems to support his belief. In a situation where he sees someone make a large donation to a charitable organization, he will credit the contribution to a tax motive. He will overlook the fact that only a portion of the contribution will be saved in actual taxes.

If a person holds a charitable, warm-hearted image of himself, he will be easily persuaded to accept arguments that are consistent with that image. This person also believes the rest of the world to be the same as himself. He recognizes, as does our hostile friend, that there are a few people different from him, but believes them to be very few in number.

Gaining Insight into How People See Themselves

Since people generally see themselves as being similar to most other people, you can gain some insight into their self-image by listening to what they say about others. As they describe others, they describe themselves. A man who says, "All men are thieves," sees himself as a thief. The exception is the person who makes prejudicial statements about a specific race or class of people other than his own race. The fact that he holds a self-image that differs from the trait that he ascribed to the group is shown by his separating himself from the group described.

People also give clues to their self-image in describing their own goals and aspirations. A person who talks about becoming a doctor in order to help people is describing a "help others" self-image. A person who talks about working himself up the corporate ladder may see himself as having a "help others" self image also. The things he describes himself doing as a corporate executive will give further clues to his self-image.

Obstacles to Idea Acceptance

Once you develop an idea of the other person's self-image, you can avoid using arguments that conflict with his self-image. The self-image is a truth to the individual. Anything that is consistent with the attitudes and beliefs making up the self-image can be accepted as true. Any idea or statement that is inconsistent with the self-image may be considered untrue.

When your idea is inconsistent with the self-image of the other person, your task is a formidable one. If that idea is inconsistent with any of the factors making up the self-image, you must find an inconsistency between his beliefs or attitudes. If your idea is worthy of the effort, you should be aware that you are attempting to change the other person's self-concept.

A person develops habits that preserve his self-image. He develops the habit of arguing against certain ideas or the habit of automatically accepting information and ideas favorable to his self-image.

If you can get the other person to change some of the protective habits he has developed, you may get him to see the logic of your viewpoint. You can do this by developing his trust. Avoid making flat assertions or flatly rejecting his arguments. You can then probe for his reasons and develop his participation in exploring the evidence you present to establish your point of view.

Overcoming Obstacles

By exploring ideas together, you have an opportunity to discuss the various possible results suggested by the evidence. By taking one point at a time, you have an opportunity to reach an agreement on small segments without using the entire argument which might challenge the other person's self-concept.

By exploring evidence in this manner, the other person learns to look at both sides of the story. He begins to see that he can explore various points of view without endangering himself. Over a period of time, he begins to change his old habits. He will begin a new habit of exploring all ideas. When the new habit is formed, he will have changed that portion of his self-image.

You can't always change the other person's mind, but you can at least be aware of the reason he is resisting your idea. You can use this knowledge to avoid making statements that you know will challenge the other person's self-image. You can also be flexible enough to change your own opinion when the other person's logic seems correct. One of the best ways to influence others is by example. If you openly admit errors and show your willingness to change your mind, it will catch on. The other person will soon begin doing the same thing.

3. DEVELOPING PSYCHOLOGICAL LEVERAGE BY BLENDING THE OTHER PERSON'S WORDS INTO YOUR CONCLUSION

People tend to accept those concepts that include their own words and ideas. If, during a discussion, you can pick out some of the words and phrases used by the other person and use them in your conclusion, you will be likely to gain acceptance and commitment.

If, for example, the person you are dealing with uses the words "honest," "integrity" and the phrases "an honest proposal," "an economically sound approach" or "a carefully developed plan," you can tie these words to your conclusion. You develop Psychological Leverage by reminding the other person, with his own words, that your idea measures up to his values. This realization results in the other person accepting your conclusion as his own.

You might present a "system change" to a person who has used these phrases by saying, "This proposal was carefully developed and is economically sound. If you give this the 'honest' effort you usually put forth, you will find it a more efficient system than the one we are now using." You are utilizing Psychological Leverage, in this example, to motivate the other person by his own words and phrases to become committed to reaching your goals.

Even on those occasions when the other person has not really offered any constructive ideas, you can still tie some of his words in to the conclusion. You can pick the part of his idea that does no harm and adjust it in some way so that it becomes useful. He will then feel that he has made a contribution and will feel committed to your conclusion.

By stating your idea in the other person's words, the idea comes alive for him. He has a better understanding of his own words and can more easily integrate the idea into his own thoughts. Again he is more likely to be committed to the idea that contains his own words.

4. HOW TO GAIN COMMITMENT BY SHARING CREDIT

I have been constantly amazed at how people will listen to your ideas one day and repeat them back to you as their own ideas the next. I have seen this happen, in some cases within an hour. Some people are unable to remember that the idea belongs to someone else and others just don't pay enough attention to determine where an idea came from. In any case, once the idea fits into a person's convictions, he begins to treat it as though it were his own.

People often strive for recognition and one way they seek recognition is by presenting ideas. You can give people recognition by giving credit for the part they play in developing solutions to the problems you work on with them. Then their commitment is assured. Commitment is always stronger to an idea that a person feels is his own or that he is gaining recognition for.

Using Involvement to Gain Commitment

I have found involvement to work equally well in family, social or business relationships. Those members of the group who were involved in developing group objectives, working on ways to achieve those objectives or working on solutions to group problems always became committed to the goals of the group. Involvement affords the opportunity to get credit at various stages which leads to commitment.

How an Objection Was Changed to Commitment. Milt, an associate marketing manager, had strong reservations about a new marketing plan that had been suggested. He was very skeptical about the project and expressed many doubts about developing it. There were many problems to be considered. Should all phases of the problem be tackled at once? How could he get support for the program? Milt had so many concerns that he felt the program could not be made to work.

Milt was asked to develop an outline that could be used to prepare the program. The outline was to include the problems that Milt saw and his ideas on preparing a guideline to overcome those problems. Milt became committed to the entire program from his involvement in developing the guideline. He began to see that the problems he thought insurmountable could be broken down and handled through the use of his guideline.

Milt's participation in developing the guideline and the credit he received as a result of his part in developing it, evoked a strong sense of accomplishment that led to his commitment to use the guideline. He became very anxious to work on the marketing program as soon as he had the guideline to follow. He was confident that his guideline would work.

Finding Specific Contributions That Are Worthy of Credit

Try to find specific contributions that the individual has made to relate to when giving credit. The more clearly the individual sees that he deserves credit the more committed he will be. Even when there is no direct contribution, however, you can always give credit for his discussing the problem with you and helping you crystalize your own ideas.

CONVERTING COMMITMENT INTO ACTION

Unfortunately, not all commitment is action oriented. We find that people may hold a belief, be committed to the principles of that belief, and yet will not take action to support it. Psychologists tell us that commitment, however, does provide a strong defense against opposing ideas. Some research has shown that people become even more committed to a belief after defending it against attack.

To get commitment converted into action, you must go beyond the techniques previously discussed. If you wish to see a subordinate, son, daughter or anyone else actively strive to achieve results from his commitment, you must provide a goal for him to work toward. If he clearly sees the goal and the steps required to achieve it, he will take action to reach the goal.

FOUR STEPS THAT INSURE ACTION

People copy successful behavior. Psychologists have found that people remember longer and emulate the behavior of a leader, if the leader received positive consequences for his behavior. This concept has been tested in sales situations and found to be an effective way to train salesmen. A sales manager played the role of a salesman making a sales presentation while the salesmen looked on.

The sales manager would use the techniques (probing, listening, etc.) that he wanted the saleman to use during a sales call. During the role play, the person playing a buyer reacted positively each time the sales manager asked a question or listened carefully.

The customer also acted out a "buy" if the overall presentation was good. The salesmen who observed these role plays were found to use the behavior demonstrated by the sales manager three times more often than salesmen who had not seen the demonstration.

Demonstrate the Action to Be Taken

The first step in converting commitment to action is to demonstrate the action that you believe will achieve your goals. Try to demonstrate the behavior in a situation that you are sure will get positive results. The behavior will be emulated and remembered longer if the positive consequences can be seen. My experience, however, shows that the behavior will be emulated, even when there is no positive consequence, if the person watching understands why there is no positive consequence.

Let the Performer Practice the Desired Action Until Comfortable

It is very important to help the other person develop a comfortable feeling in performing new activities. People tend to exercise behavior that they are familiar with. Their old patterns are familiar and comfortable and they will utilize the old ones until they feel comfortable with the new behaviors.

You may have to walk through the activity with the other person. If the situation is one that permits "role play," this is an excellent way to practice. Three is the magic number for learning a new activity or behavior. If you can get a person to act out a certain behavior three times, he will feel comfortable in using the new behavior. Acting out the behavior has also been found, by psychologists, to intensify commitment to the new behavior.

Provide the Performer Some Freedom of Choice

The third step in converting commitment into activity is to provide some freedom of choice. If you can offer alternative courses of action, the other person can then choose what, for him, looks best. He already will have seen a successful example and has practiced a successful method of behavior. He will probably choose the method demonstrated.

Develop a Written Action Plan

An action plan, the fourth step, identifies a specific objective, outlines the steps to be taken, specifies the techniques to be employed, is time-related and can be evaluated. The action plan is widely used in business to direct activities. This same method can be used in any situation to convert commitment into action.

The action plan, in effect, becomes a contract between you and the other person. By getting his proposed activities listed in writing, he has a constant reminder of the agreement and the procedure he is to follow. Often people forget the reasons or the steps they are to take in accomplishing a goal. This written plan eliminates that possibility.

Putting a plan in writing also crystalizes the elements of the plan in the person's mind. If, as he writes, he feels uncomfortable with some part of the plan, it can be changed. Once he has written it and is in agreement with the plan, he becomes even more committed to pursuing the plan.

HOW TO DETERMINE THE OTHER PERSON'S LEVEL OF COMMITMENT

An easy way to determine a person's level of commitment is to ask him to summarize his intended actions. If you can get the other person to tell you what action he intends to take, you get a glimpse of how dedicated he is to the idea. If he is highly committed, he will probably give you specific details and an immediate timetable. If he is not really committed to action, he will find it difficult to enumerate his plans.

If the other person is not committed to any action, you can lead him into a discussion of what would be appropriate action. Once this has been done, ask him to summarize what would be effective. The fact that he vocalizes the actions that would be effective may result in his use of the behavior discussed.

In business situations, of course, this summary can become the basis for the other person's written objectives. He may not be completely committed, but he will understand what is expected of him. The summary provides a base to use in evaluating his performance at a later date.

How One Unit Manager Doubled His Profit in One Year. The manager of a Southwestern distribution center was facing a problem of low morale, poor profits and an inefficient warehousing operation. This manager, Tom, had just recently been assigned to the center. His predecessor had experienced large losses every month during the previous six months.

Tom had made some progress during his first month, due to his direct intervention in the warehousing operation. Now, he needed to build morale and develop a smoothly operating management group which would be committed to getting the job done. He found his opportunity to stimulate the group while reviewing the results of one of the other company distribution centers.

One of the centers, the Southern center, was making more money than Tom's, yet it had only half the number of people. Tom developed a theme that was to double his profit in less than a year. He called a meeting of his management team and discussed their problems. Then he gave them the information on the Southern center Tom suggested that they should be able to double the results of the Southern center.

The theme, "Double the Southern center," became the rallying cry. No one could argue with the idea that double the number of people should be able to double the results. Soon every member of the team was echoing Tom's call to "Double the Southern center's results."

Tom had found a "superordinate" goal. Everyone had something to try for that was higher and more important than his own individual problems. Soon everyone was committed to the goal of doubling the Southern center's results.

During the following three months, productivity increased rapidly. The costs of operating dropped and profits started to increase. The increased profits provided positive reinforcement for the group. The product sales managers started getting new business and this resulted in additional efficiency in operations. Within three months, Tom had led his unit far past the profits of the Southern center.

Tom then started working with each sales manager to develop action plans to continue their progress. Tom made sales calls with the sales managers and demonstrated the "no-nonsense" management approach that he wanted utilized. He helped the sales managers prepare their presentations and practiced with them. He solicited their ideas and used them.

Every month the business grew By the end of the ninth month they were doing eighty per cent more business than the Southern center. Tom rewarded each individual team member for his contribution. He congratulated them as a group and gave individual credit for improved sales and operations performance.

Tom may or may not have known it, but he followed proven psychological principles in developing a high level of commitment to a goal. Each individual was able to see how his personal goals meshed with the overriding organizational goals.

During the eleventh month, Tom had a meeting with his management team and announced that they had achieved their goal. Their monthly profit was running double the Southern center's. Everyone cheered. Every manager in that room knew that he had done his part. Morale was higher than it had ever been before. Someone asked, "What are we going to do next year, as an encore?" Tom replied, "I think we ought to double our own profits next year." And that became the guideline for a new objective that was eventually accomplished.

The following checklist will insure the kind of commitment that Tom developed in his distribution center:

1 Tie your ideas to the other person's motivations.
2. Tie your ideas to the other person's self-image.
3. Blend the other person's words and ideas into the conclusion.
4. Let the other person take part of the credit.

Then convert that commitment into action by:

5. Demonstrating the activity that will accomplish the goal.
6 Helping the other person become comfortable in performing the new activity.
7. Providing for some freedom of choice of actions.
8. Developing written action plans.

Leverage Techniques That Win People's Minds

You can increase your Psychological Leverage, enhance the power of your words and effectively use what you say to win the minds of all the people you deal with each day. In this chapter you will learn the secret that all true leaders have used to win power and influence. You will see how helping other people increases your influence, develops admiration and wins respect and trust.

I'll show you discussion techniques that help people solve problems, build self-confidence and openly express their views. You will learn to improve your own results by evoking creativity from others. You can use these techniques to enhance your prestige and expand your Psychological Leverage in dealing with people.

Just as the great leaders throughout history have won the minds of the people who supported them, you can win the minds of the people with whom you deal. Whether it is one person or a group, a child or an adult, a friend or a stranger, the technique is the same. The secret is to "zero in" on their needs and problems. You win their minds by helping them solve the problems that impede their progress.

TWO WAYS TO HELP PEOPLE SOLVE PROBLEMS

You can help people solve their problems by helping them develop confidence in their own abilities and by getting them to express their own ideas and opinions. Both of these goals can be accomplished through discussion. The discussion techniques of probing and active listening have been tested in hundreds of business, social and family situations and found effective in developing confidence and in evoking ideas and opinions that lead to the solutions of people's problems.

As they express their ideas and feelings they clarify their own thoughts. As they see their problems more clearly they see more ways to resolve them. The knowledge that they are seeing the problem more clearly and that there are some logical ways to solve it helps them develop self-confidence. They see that they can work out their own problems.

1. HOW TO HELP PEOPLE BUILD SELF-CONFIDENCE

Psychologists have found that a sympathetic understanding will bring about change in other people. You can help them change and become more self-confident by trying to see the situation from the other person's point of view. If you can develop the empathy to sense how the other person feels and understand his frame of reference, he will begin to change. He will listen to himself, clarify his thinking and develop more confidence in his ability to think and express himself.

Using Active Listening

One way to help people build self-confidence is to use active listening during discussion. As you listen, you can encourage the other person to express his thoughts and opinions. If some part of what is said is not clear to you, it probably is not clear to the person speaking to you. By asking the other person questions for clarification, you actually help him clarify his own thoughts. When the statements are clarified, respond immediately. Offer immediate encouragement, summarize what the individual has said and offer praise when an improvement is made. This immediate favorable response will encourage further attempts at clarification and increase self-confidence.

Redirecting People's Efforts

Another way to help people develop self-confidence is to redirect their efforts from short- to long-range goals. Often people who lack self-confidence are concentrating on short range goals. They expect to accomplish some goal in a few weeks or a few months, when actually it might take six months or more to acquire the knowledge or skills necessary for completing the goal. Each time an individual attempts a goal that he is not prepared for, he will fail if he does not allow time to acquire the necessary knowledge or skills. Repeated failures, due to these "short run" goals, block the development of self-confidence.

You can help an individual who lacks self-confidence eliminate these barriers by encouraging him to acquire long-range goals. By concentrating on long-range goals, which encourages the building of longer term expectations, people will persist for longer periods of time in seeking their goals. Since the ultimate goal is expected at some point in the future, the individual will have time to develop the needed skills before he loses confidence in himself. With time available the individual can learn the skills in small, successive steps. As he successfully completes each step, he sees that he is capable of learning and he builds his self-confidence slowly and surely.

Building Confidence Through Group Activities

Another way to build self-confidence is through membership in a group with high morale. If a group is successful in its activities, each group member feels partly responsible for the success and feels self-confident in the group atmosphere. This feeling carries over into other similar activities and becomes a base for an individual's overall confidence in himself. You can encourage a person who lacks self-confidence to join such a group or you can help develop high morale in a group he is already a member of.

Providing Easy Tasks

Since self-confidence is based upon previous success, you can help a person or a group by providing a series of tasks that are easy to complete. After the person has developed a success record, make the tasks more difficult. Keep each series of tasks easy in relation to the previously completed series. The person will develop more self-confidence as he completes each series of tasks.

Even in the completion of easy tasks, people who are generally submissive will need more structure and guidance. They need the constant support of someone they trust at each stage of their learning. Leaving them completely free to develop their own techniques will cause them to become anxious and less and less confident of their abilities.

You can help submissive people build confidence by guiding

them slowly and surely. Make sure they become completely familiar with each step, completely confident, before going on to the next. Keep them aware that you, or someone, will always be there to help them when they need help.

Reinforcing Success with Praise

You can provide the reinforcement that people need to develop self-confidence by giving praise and understanding. If you constantly praise those actions that are truly deserving of praise, the individual will feel good about his success and begin to feel self-confident. The positive feedback shows him that he is successful in the eyes of others. You can also offer positive feedback when he fails, by providing words of understanding and encouragement. Show that you think he will be successful if he keeps trying.

2. HOW TO BRING OUT IDEAS AND OPINIONS THAT SOLVE PROBLEMS

You can evoke the ideas and opinions that may solve an individual's problems through questioning. Questioning techniques not only bring surface opinions out, they also incite mental activity that culminates in more profound ideas and opinions.

Questions That Stimulate Problem Solving

You can guide a person to the solution of his problems by asking questions that cause him to evaluate various alternatives that may solve his problem. By asking how "X" affects the problem or what would happen if "Y" were used, you cause the individual to evaluate alternatives and look at different parts of the problem.

Questioning will also stimulate problem solving on the part of people who are usually defensive. Defensive people generally are afraid of being criticized or evaluated. So, when questioning them, show them that they will not be criticized or evaluated.

A Training Group That Helped Solve a Problem. I attended a training workshop in which a number of trainers were discussing their plans for the coming year. One of the trainers was new and had been given what he described as "an impossible task." All of his company's employees were to be given an orientation to the various activities performed by the six divisions of the company. The trainer was to write an orientation that would acquaint all employees with the main function of each division.

The trainer had absolutely no confidence in his ability to develop a program that would cover the needs of all these people who had such divergent backgrounds. He complained that "there was no way to write one program to fit three different groups."

First, the other trainers listened and asked questions for clarification. They then expressed understanding for the magnitude of the problem. (Active listening.) Questions were asked to determine the make-up of the various groups and the information that each group needed. Slowly the new trainer began to think clearly and finally expressed the problem in clear and specific terms.

The problem was that about fifty per cent of the employees were new and had no knowledge of the functions performed by the various divisions. The other fifty per cent were long tenure employees who had a great deal of knowledge about many of the divisions but very little knowledge about one or two of the newer divisions. Each employee's knowledge was basically limited to the particular divisions he worked with.

Next, the other trainers asked questions to elicit the new trainer's opinion on how to develop an orientation program for the new employees. The new trainer saw this as an easy task and quickly explained a logical approach.

The new trainer was praised for his quick solution to this portion of the problem. The praise helped him develop self-confidence and he quickly tackled the problem of developing a separate program for the long tenure employees.

By careful questioning the trainers influenced the new trainer so that he examined the "impossible task" in small segments that became easy tasks. As he successfully resolved each easy task, he became more and more self-confident.

Finally, the new trainer saw that the solution was to develop a program composed of a general orientation session for all employees, followed by six divisional sessions. Each employee would select and attend the divisional sessions in which he needed information. The importance of the solution is not how the problem was solved, but rather that the new trainer solved the problem himself.

TWO WAYS TO DEVELOP CREATIVITY

You can win the trust, confidence, respect and admiration of people by helping them bring out their own creativity. As they begin to see the value in creative solutions to their problems they will place more value on your advice. You can use the techniques developed here to guide them toward the creative accomplishment of their goals.

1. A TEN-POINT CREATIVITY GUIDELINE

Creativity is fostered in an atmosphere of understanding and permissiveness. You can encourage creativity and develop your own Psychological Leverage by creating conditions of permissiveness. You can use an understanding of the creative process to direct people's activities in such a way that the conditions you develop evoke creativity.

Many researchers have studied the creative process and have offered various explanations of how it works. Creativity is the evolution of a new element such as a new idea, technique or action through the transformation of one element or the integration of two or more separate elements. According to the researchers, these transformations take place when a person, seeking the solution to a problem, mentally superimposes one or more unusual elements over one another or over elements of a problem.

Creativity results from unusual associations and is more prevalent in situations where goals are actively pursued. The more associations that are made, the more likely the solutions are to be creative.

A number of attempts have been made to develop a systematic approach to creativity. A synthesis of various problem-solving and creativity approaches are presented here as a creativity guideline that you can use in developing Psychological Leverage and winning the minds of people.

1. Write a statement of a goal or problem in general terms.
2. Break the general problem down into the probable causes or obstacles to the solution.
3. Restate the problem or goal in specific terms which encompass the main causes or the largest obstacles to a solution.
4. Develop as many alternative approaches to solving the problem as possible.
5. Form associations between the alternatives by picking elements from each alternative and combining it with an element of each of the other alternatives.
6. Form pictures of the associations. The pictures need not be sensible or rational.
7. Modify the pictures by changing the structure or size of the elements, rearranging the elements or changing the pattern. Look for the unusual or ridiculous as you modify the picture.

8. Stop working on the problem for an hour or more. Some writers suggest discussing a completely irrelevant subject during this break. The irrelevant subject is then used later to form new associations with the previously developed alternatives.
9. Develop a new list of alternative solutions based on the associations that have been developed.
10. Test the solutions against probable consequences and select the one most likely to succeed.

During the early months of World War II, German submarines were sinking American ships with virtual immunity from reprisals. Hundreds of American lives and millions of dollars in ships and cargo were being lost to the unrelenting submarine attacks. A special group of intellectuals was brought together by the U.S. government to form a "think tank" to find a creative solution to the "submarine" problem.

The group established their problem statement as "Stop the German submarines." Under pressure to find an immediate solution, the group was unproductive and lost valuable time. Their lists of obstacles and alternatives were unproductive. Their usual problem-solving techniques failed. Then one of the group members raised the opinion that "This problem is so ridiculous that it will take a ridiculous solution." That remark led to a solution that created confusion, uncertainty and frustration all the way up to the German High Command.

The "think tank" group tossed off the constraints of convention. They began to look at the unusual and the ridiculous, they modified the problem. They changed the elements and structure of the problem to completely irrelevant situations, such as trying to get a submarine out of a house or trying to stop the clock, until the attacking submarine could be found and sunk.

They superimposed one element over another, such as a clock spring spread over the ocean in an expanded form. Finally the solution evolved.

A search pattern was developed that virtually guaranteed the blocking of the escape of any detected submarine. The search pattern was one similar to an expanding circular clock spring. By expanding the circle in relation to the speed of a submarine, the submarine could theoretically never get outside the search pattern. So many submarines were sunk by this method that the German High Command believed we had broken their codes or developed some new secret weapon. This same creative system that helped shorten the war, can be learned and used by anyone.

2. HOW TO USE THE CREATIVITY GUIDELINE TO HELP OTHERS

You can follow the creativity guideline in guiding the activities of people whom you are trying to help. If you are dealing with students or people who are under your direction in an organization, you can assign tasks and direct their activities so that they must go through the ten steps of the creativity guideline to reach the assigned goals.

In dealing with people who are not under your direction, you must persuade through suggestion and lead through questioning. You can suggest that steps one through three be followed and then ask questions to lead them through the remaining steps. You might ask, "What are some other alternatives?" for step four. Other questions are: For step six, "What would that look like if you could picture it?" For step seven, "How would that work if we reversed the elements?" In step ten, "What would the consequences be if we tried this alternative?"

The following steps will be helpful in assigning and directing the activities of people in such a way that their efforts will achieve more creative results.

1. Provide an atmosphere of freedom to experiment without criticism.
2. Require written statements of objectives or problems.
3. Require the individual to discuss the problem with three or four people whose divergent backgrounds may provide different viewpoints on the problem.
4. Frequently ask the individual for reports. Ask for a summary of each divergent viewpoint encountered.
5. Ask what part of each divergent idea is good.
6. Ask for a written report listing all possible alternatives.
7. Ask that the individual take a day or two away from the problem and then look for additional solutions.
8. Ask for his decision.

By guiding people through these eight steps you will get double leverage here, in that the results they get make you look better and at the same time you win their minds for helping them. The respect and admiration that people hold for you as a result of your efforts to help in their self-development, leads to more cooperation and greater efforts on their part to support your goals.

HOW TO DEVELOP A CREATIVE ENVIRONMENT

Psychologists and other researchers have shown that creativity is fostered in an atmosphere of permissiveness and understanding. When people feel that their ideas, opinions and errors are understood, they are free from the frustrations that block their creativity. In an atmosphere of permissiveness, people feel free to spontaneously express any idea that comes to mind. When this freedom for spontaneity exists, there will be a lot of uncertainty about what is going to be said at any time.

When people feel free to spontaneously say whatever they please, they often say things that are unexpected. As unexpected statements are made by one person, another person will spontaneously form associations that are unexpected and often respond creatively. The individual would block these creative expressions and respond in the normally expected way, if he did not feel free to express any irrelevant statement he chose to make.

There are ten conditions that have been found to evoke creativity. You can promote these ten conditions to help people become more creative and more productive. The ten conditions are:

1. Provide a clearly defined goal to work toward.
2. Instill a high expectation of success.
3. Demonstrate a high level of trust.
4. Encourage complete freedom of speech.
5. Do not criticize any idea or suggestion.
6. Encourage the clarification of ideas.
7. Encourage interdependence.
8. Thoroughly explore irrelevant ideas.
9. Encourage self-assessment.
10. Promote individual psychological growth.

1. PROVIDE A CLEARLY DEFINED GOAL

By accepting a goal, an individual assumes the responsibility for achieving that goal. Often people get off the track and use the wrong techniques or follow pathways that do not lead to the accomplishment of the goal. They make errors and hinder their own progress. You can help them avoid many of these errors or misdirected efforts by making certain that their goal is clearly defined. Clearly defined goals keep people on the track and reduce the possibility of errors. The first three steps of the Creativity Guideline provide a system for clearly defining problems or goals. You can use those three steps to help others develop a clear guideline for the achievement of their goals.

2. INSTILL A HIGH EXPECTATION OF SUCCESS

Research has shown that people do better, achieve higher goals and are more successful generally when they hold high expectations of success. One way that people develop high expectations is through the assimilation of the expectations of their peers and superiors. Children and young adults, in trying to please their parents, assume the goals of the parents. People in general assume the goals and expectations of peer groups and people in higher social and business positions. You can utilize this tendency for people to assume the expectations of people they admire by demonstrating that you expect great results.

You can set high goals and demonstrate your confidence in a person's ability to achieve those goals. To develop this high expectation you can build a series of small successes to refer to. An individual tends to develop confidence in his abilities in relation to the positive feedback he receives. So, establish a number of sub-goals or smaller goals that lead up to the big goal and dwell on the successes. You may also refer to past successes as an additional means of supporting your reasons for believing that he will attain the high goals you set.

Be positive and stick to your campaign to instill confidence, but make sure your statements are logical. Do not exaggerate. State your reasons for believing he can succeed, provide feedback in specific terms and show him the progress he is making. As the progress improves and the evidence mounts, he will assume the same expectations that you hold. Your faith in him will pay off by his having more faith in you.

3. DEMONSTRATE A HIGH LEVEL OF FAITH

Someone coined the term "The self-fulfilling prophesy" to describe the effect your beliefs about a person will have on his behavior. If you believe a person is highly trustworthy, you unconsciously treat him as a highly trustworthy person. He then responds to your faith in a highly trustworthy way. Most people want to exhibit highly valued characteristics and will show them at the slightest encouragement. As long as you demonstrate a high level of faith in another person, that person will try to live up to your expectations.

On the other hand, if you believe a person cannot be trusted, you will unconsciously demonstrate your distrust. The other person, sensing your distrust, will feel resentful because he is being wrongly suspected. There is no motivation to continue being trustworthy when your efforts are not recognized. The distrusted person will often stop conducting himself in a trustworthy manner, because he sees that his trustworthiness is not recognized. The self-fulfilling prophecy works in both instances. The other person responds to your actions which unconsciously reflect your beliefs.

4. ENCOURAGE COMPLETE FREEDOM OF SPEECH

Some of the most creative ideas evolve in casual conversation. As long as everyone feels completely free to express any view he holds, there is a high chance of creativity through cross fertilization of ideas. When people feel they have to modify their speech to fit the rules and regulations of the organization they stick to the standard accepted statements and block their own creative ability. You can overcome these barriers by encouraging free speech in all situations.

5. AVOID CRITICISM

When people are criticized they tend to stop contributing or they only discuss safe topics. If you feel someone is trying to lead the conversation astray or if his idea is not appropriate, don't criticize it. Ask the person to write the idea out for later discussion. Point out that it may be important for another part of the problem. Redirect the conversation to the original point by stating that you want to look at one particular part of the problem now. You can also redirect the conversation by asking a question. You might ask how someone feels about a certain part of the problem. Or, you might ask for someone else's comments after suggesting the previous comment be written out and saved for later discussion.

You can also redirect people who come up with inappropriate suggestions by saying that they seem to be ahead of you and you would like to discuss their idea when you get to that point, but you would like to explore the current element first.

6. HOW TO ENCOURAGE THE CLARIFICATION OF IDEAS

Often people have good ideas but don't express them very well. The more they talk the more they get away from their real point. When this occurs, stay with the idea until you get it expressed in a clear and concise way. Keep asking the individual questions until he restates the idea in a way that everyone understands. You may ask others to comment on the idea and then ask the original speaker to relate to the comments. Eventually the original speaker will clarify his own thoughts or someone will come up with a clarification that he accepts. Often during a discussion for clarification, a new, more creative idea will emerge due to someone misunderstanding or seeing the original statement differently.

7. HOW TO ENCOURAGE INTERDEPENDENCE

It has been proven time and again that interdependence is more fruitful than independent actions. When the diverse knowledge of two or more people is intermingled, better solutions evolve. No one person has enough knowledge to know the best solution for every situation. One single idea expressed by one person often triggers new insight on the part of others. The new insight when expressed then triggers additional insight on the part of someone else. Encourage those with whom you deal to discuss their ideas with other people. This discussion will expose them to knowledge that they may have overlooked. Often they emerge with more creative ideas than they had originally.

8. EXPLORING IRRELEVANT IDEAS

Creativity is the development of something new. Most often the creativity comes from an irrelevant fact or idea. At first glance, the irrelevant idea may have no value but upon closer examination, a part may be found that is relevant to the problem. When an irrelevant suggestion or idea is proposed, ask questions about every element of the suggestion until you are sure there is no way to use it. As you discuss each element, ask how the idea could be used as opposed to asking if it can be used.

By asking how an idea can be used, you are directing their mental energies toward the development of a solution that combines the individual elements. This provides the Psychological Leverage of searching for a way to do it, of problem solving, rather than evaluating it.

9. ENCOURAGE SELF-ASSESSMENT

People often go through the motions but do not really think about what they are doing. One of the biggest problems in training people is to get them to think about the information they are working with. Many people want to sit passively and have the new techniques appear in their minds. The same problem exists in trying to get people to think creatively. You need to bring to their attention the need to apply some energy, to try to think and to assess their efforts.

Ask them to stop and analyze what they are doing. Ask if they are thinking of how they have solved other problems. Are they thinking of similar and contrasting usages and ideas? Are they comparing the new idea with ideas they have used before? Are they combining the new parts with old parts? Are they trying to picture what the new system would look like? Or are they passively sitting and waiting for something to happen?

10. HOW TO PROMOTE INDIVIDUAL PSYCHOLOGICAL GROWTH

The psychologist Abraham Maslow believed that the one common thread to creativity was psychological growth. As man matures, as he becomes less defensive and more open and cooperative, he becomes more creative. You can help others grow and become more creative by involving them with other people. You can bring them into discussions of problems and objectives that you are working on. You can solicit their participation in your projects and plans. All of these participation techniques coupled with a creative environment will promote psychological growth

How a Foreman Used Employee Development to Reduce Work Problems. Bill Jackson, a newly appointed general foreman for a manufacturing plant, was facing a serious problem. Nearly half the people he supervised had been transferred to Bill from an older plant that had been closed. Many of these employees were bitter and depressed because of the change. Some of them had been supervisors at the old plant, but had to be downgraded in order to transfer to the new plant.

The transferred employees did not perform "up to standard," showed little enthusiasm for their work and started to have a negative effect on the older workers. The older workers were still performing well, but had picked up the tendency to "gripe" from the new workers.

Bill initiated an employee development program in the hope of overcoming the depressed feelings that many workers had. Their preoccupation with bitterness and depression was slowing down the employees. Bill's idea was to overcome the depressed feelings by giving the employees new confidence and pride in their work skills.

Bill offered each employee the opportunity to work on a new machine for one hour each day, until he mastered the new machine. The senior machine operator would decide when the trainee had learned enough to operate the new machine full time. At that point, the new operator would be certified. There would have to be an even exchange between departments, so that all machines would be kept working. Any person could continue training until he was certified on all machines. Once a person became certified for any machine, he could request a temporary or permanent change to the new machine.

There was some initial "griping," but as the first few men began to train on new machines, interest developed. When the first certificates were awarded, the interest developed into enthusiasm. Bill complimented the people who learned the new machines and encouraged others to do the same. Bill put a chart on the wall that showed the number of machines each employee could operate.

Bill also encouraged those who learned the new machines to discuss the differences in the machines on their breaks and at lunch time. Slowly Bill let it be known that he expected every employee to eventually operate every machine. He talked about how productivity would increase and praised the operators who had learned the new machines for leading the way.

Bill added another chart to the wall, one that showed his productivity goals. He filled in the production figures each week, so the employees could see where they stood in relation to their goals.

Bill's plan worked. As the employees concentrated on learning new machines, they became interested in doing better on their old ones. As their skills increased, their self-confidence increased and from that self-confidence came enthusiasm.

Bill reached his goal. He helped his subordinates overcome their depression and apathy toward their work. He helped them become more skilled at their jobs. He helped them develop new confidence and reach for higher goals. He won their trust and respect. They achieved the production goals to please Bill and eventually surpassed them to please themselves.

10

Winning Trust and Confidence: A Sure Way to Double the Power of What You Say

You can expand your influence on more and more people by earning their trust and confidence. As people see that you can be trusted, they tend to accept your ideas and follow your suggestions. In this chapter, you will see how to double the power of what you say by using discussion techniques that win people's trust and confidence.

First you'll see specific discussion techniques that can help you win the trust of others. Then I'll cover the importance of voice patterns in winning trust. I will show how self-disclosure immediately increases your power to evoke information from other people. You will learn speaking techniques that have been tested and proven effective in thousands of discussions between people in everyday situations.

By practicing the techniques covered in this chapter, you will be able to speak in a warm and pleasing manner. Your voice itself will inspire confidence. You will be able to display assertiveness, confidence, honesty and trustworthiness. You will learn to blend warmth and concern for the other person with candor and assertiveness. As you practice, your Psychological Leverage will grow and you'll double the power of what you say.

DISCUSSION TECHNIQUES THAT WIN TRUST

The purpose of discussion is to fulfill the human need to express our feelings, beliefs, emotional reactions and our opinions to another human being. We might speculate that the first word invented by man grew out of his desire to verbally express some great grief, joy or anger. When words are used for their intended purpose, to express feelings and opinions, they are accepted and trusted. How can you doubt or distrust someone who begins his commentary with, "I feel," or "In my opinion"? Since his statements are not presented as irrefutable fact, there is nothing to doubt or distrust.

How to Develop Speech Techniques That Promote Trust

Doubt and distrust begin to surface in people's minds when we present our point of view as an irrefutable fact. Many people, in their attempts to persuade others to see things or do things their way, present their views or their evidence as unchallengeable laws or irrefutable evidence. This aggressive speaking style, in most situations, results in the loss of trust. In my opinion, there is a direct relationship between verbal aggression and the lack of trust. The relationship may be expressed as follows: *As one person's verbal aggressiveness increases, the other person's trust in the aggressive speaker decreases.*

The most easily learned and yet most important discussion technique is to express the points you wish to make as your opinions, ideas or feelings. If those ideas, opinions and feelings seem reasonable and logical to the other person, they will be accepted. If you present them in a verbally aggressive way, however, they will be rejected due to distrust, even though they may seem reasonable and logical. The utilization of Psychological Leverage, through the development of trust, occurs due to "how you say it," more than from what you say.

How to Show That You Can Be Trusted

The second most important discussion technique that wins trust from other people is the development of good listening habits. After you express an opinion or idea, listen carefully to the other person's response. Weigh what he says against your intended meaning. When differences occur, find out whether he misunderstood you or holds a different viewpoint. A misunderstanding can be cleared up by stating your view in a different way. But when the other person holds a different view, you can win his trust by asking for more information, listening carefully and sincerely trying to understand his point of view. Good listening techniques show the other person that he can trust you to fairly evaluate his ideas. This trust carries over when he is evaluating what you say.

I have found that good listening habits are especially effective in calming people who tend to become excited when presenting their point of view. When my children reached their teen-age years, they began to argue more forcefully to support their point of view. Occasionally they became excited during a discussion and raised their voices in what seemed to be anger.

At first I reacted to their excitement with sharp criticism. I refused to let them express anger in supporting their opinions. This suppression of their feelings led to real anger, resentment and hurt feelings. Later I discovered that their excitement reflected enthusiasm rather than anger.

I then found that by listening carefully and honestly trying to understand their point of view, their excitement waned. As soon as they saw that I was really listening, they calmed down. They lowered their voice as they realized that they could trust me to listen to what they had to say.

How to Use Voice Techniques That Promote Trust

You can also win trust from other people by slightly altering the tone, volume, rate of speech and the emotional quality of your voice. Our voices reveal the feelings or emotions that we experience and people make judgements about our trustworthiness based upon these revelations. By learning voice qualities that indicate trustworthiness, you can leave a more favorable impression.

Speech therapists discovered, and professional speaking organizations later tested and practiced, voice techniques that expressed warmth, concern for others, empathy and sincerity, which lead people to trust the speaker. Other voice techniques were also identified that caused people to feel distrust for the speaker.

You can begin your program of building trust by speaking in a relaxed way with quiet words. If you can develop a relaxed attitude, your warmth and concern for people will show through. You can develop a relaxed attitude by acting relaxed. People generally can not tell that you are not relaxed unless you become so nervous that your hands shake or your voice cracks. You can overcome these extreme problems by clenching your fists and then relaxing them and by taking slow deep breaths.

Empathy can build trust if it is clearly shown. You can show empathy for people by slowing your rate of speaking and by speaking in a calm relaxed way. To hear some extreme examples of empathy being shown through speech, listen to any mother talking to a new baby. The baby doesn't understand the words, yet it responds to the tenderness and love that the mother expresses through the use of sound.

The quality of the sounds you make reveals your feelings about the people you are talking to. The quality may be affected by tension. A harsh, guttural sound, which irritates many people, may be caused by nervousness and tension. You can improve the quality of your voice and develop more pleasing sounds by relaxing. Just try to feel friendly, act confident and present your ideas with enthusiasm and eagerness.

"Characteristics of People I'll Trust and Listen To"

In addition to the voice modulation and discussion techniques presented in this chapter, there are a number of other characteristics that will help you develop trust and double the power of what you say. The following list is one of two lists developed by more than two hundred people who gave the characteristics of people they did or did not trust and listen to. The first list covers characteristics of people the two hundred respondents said they would trust and listen to.

1. Has a sound knowledge of the subject.
2. Has a friendly attitude toward other people.
3. Sincere and honest.
4. Has a pleasant tone of voice.
5. An authority on the subject.
6. An authority in another field.
7. Clear and concise.
8. Enthusiastic and eager to communicate.
9. Dynamic in vocal expression.
10. Presents new information or a new application for known information.
11. Respectful.
12. Relates to personal experiences of audience.
13. States an economic, social or philosophical impact of his proposal.
14. Promotes discussion.
15. Encourages participation.

"Characteristics of People That I Tend To Distrust and Avoid Listening To"

The following list was developed at the same time by the same two hundred people and characterizes people whom they would not trust and would avoid listening to:

1. Repetitious.
2. Autocratic
3. Demanding
4. Not serious.
5. Talks over your head.
6. Boring.
7. Critical.
8. Speaks in a monotone.
9. Wanders away from topic.
10. Interrupts other people.
11. No eye-contact.
12. Not prepared.
13. Not interesting.
14. Speaks too fast.
15. Leaves no room for questions.
16. Doesn't state importance of topic.
17. Uses examples that don't relate to topic.
18. Doesn't listen to the responses.
19. Doesn't clearly state his purpose.
20. Uses inappropriate jokes.

How an Interview Changed a Dissatisfied Employee. Phillip Marks didn't like his boss, was dissatisfied with his job and was looking for a new one. This information was brought to the attention of Joe Bliss, the personnel manager. Joe called Phil into his office to discuss Phil's feelings about the job.

Joe explained that he had heard rumors that Phil was leaving and would like to find out what problems had caused him to make this decision. Joe listened patiently as Phil explained his problem. Phil felt that he was not getting ahead fast enough. He felt that after eighteen months on the job he should be a supervisor. He also felt that his boss was giving him all the irritating jobs to do. He felt he did all the dirty work and his boss got all the credit.

After listening carefully, Joe expressed understanding for Phil's feelings, based upon Phil's beliefs about the job and his boss. Joe then expressed his own views *as opinions, in a non-critical way*. Joe candidly pointed out that eighteen months was not acceptable to management as enough experience to be promoted to a supervisory position. Joe also offered the opinion that the dirty jobs were his boss' way of training him for a supervisory position. He suggested that Phil take and read a "position description" for the supervisory job and compare his job assignments with the areas of responsibility he would have as a supervisor.

Phil came back to see Joe the following week with a changed attitude. He now saw that he needed more time to prepare for the supervisory position and expressed a great deal of trust and confidence in Joe. Joe had earned this trust by his non-critical, yet candid, expression of his opinions, by listening and empathizing with Phil and by letting Phil make up his own mind.

THE PSYCHOLOGY OF CONFIDENCE

To gain a person's confidence is to go beyond trust. If someone trusts you, it means that he expects you to act in a specified way, if and when you act. If you do not act or do not achieve the desired results, you lose nothing and you are still trustworthy. You may trust someone to act honestly without any expectation as to when an action will occur.

Confidence includes an expectation that an action will take place, that a specific action will be performed or that a specific result will be achieved. For example, you may feel confident that your spouse will voluntarily tell people of your high level of integrity. You may trust a friend to tell one of your favorable characteristics, when asked. You may feel confident that your spouse will do so whether asked or not.

You can improve your Psychological Leverage in dealing with people by acting in such a way that people develop a high level of confidence in what you do and say. The three main factors that have been found to be the basis for confidence are confidentiality, candor and assertiveness

The Confidentiality Factor

The quickest way to destroy the confidence that an individual has in you is to repeat things that you were told to keep secret. In spite of the certainty of losing people's respect and confidence, telling a secret is the most common violation of all human contracts. We know most people are honorable and would not intentionally break a confidence, so why does this happen?

One reason people break confidences is that they forget and tell or they let it slip out during casual conversation. They seem to let their guard down during conversation and give away the secret before they realize what they have done. Once they have let the information out, they feel sorry and many report their error to the person they had promised secrecy.

Most violations occur, however, because the person violating the trust did not realize that the information was confidential. Either he didn't listen carefully or the other person didn't clearly state that the information was to be kept secret. Regardless of who erred, the person who lets the information out will lose the confidence of the other person.

You can build a reputation as being a person who will keep a secret under any circumstances. As people become aware of this reputation, they will begin to trust and have confidence in you. To build this reputation, you must take the burden of responsibility totally upon yourself. You must make sure in all cases that anything told to you is not confidential prior to revealing it.

The easiest way to be sure that you never violate a confidence is to continually check your sources of information to ascertain the confidentiality of any information they have given you. Unless you can specifically remember being told that the information is not confidential, don't pass it on. When in doubt, keep it secret. Many times your memory may fail and you may withhold information that is not confidential, but you won't lose confidence by erring on the side of caution.

Slips of the tongue, as well as forgetting, will cease once you develop the determination to keep information confidential that has been entrusted to you as confidential information. If you start to slip, your subconscious mind will come to your rescue. Once you have firmly planted in your mind that you will not reveal confidential information, your subconscious mind will guide you away from the error of revealing confidential information.

How to Use Candor to Win Confidence

When people find out that some individual has not leveled with them, they lose confidence in that person. No one really wants to be flattered, for example, or told that he is more intelligent, proficient or capable than he really is. If you tell children or adults that they are doing excellent work, they become satisfied and stop striving for improvement. If they later see others doing much better work, they realize that you are either not being candid with them or that you are not capable of evaluating their progress. In either case you lose their confidence.

You can gain or hold another's confidence by candidly stating exactly what you believe. You can do this without rejecting or attacking the other person. If the person feels his ego threatened, he may reject a candid appraisal. You can avoid threatening the individual by explaining that his progress is satisfactory for the period of time involved, but that his level of proficiency is still below the level you expect him to eventually reach.

When dealing with behavioral problems, such as sarcastic remarks, interrupting or other obnoxious behavior, point out some other socially acceptable behavior for comparison. Remind him of the better results he achieved when using the more acceptable behavior. Be careful to indicate your understanding and acceptance and explain that you are only offering your candid opinion on ways to get better results.

One of the most rewarding experiences for members of Toastmaster's Clubs is the candid evaluation they receive from fellow club members after they make a speech. Club members bring the speaker's attention to both his weak and strong points. He can then strengthen his strong points and concentrate on improving his weaknesses.

I have seen a number of people who actually shook with fear when first trying to speak. After a few candid evaluations by club members, they were able to speak without any visible nervousness. They trusted the club members enough to follow their advice.

How to Use Assertiveness to Develop Confidence

Every decision you make affects the confidence people have in you. Every action you take leads to more confidence. Each time you stand up for someone, others develop confidence in you. Every time you take an assertive position that confidence grows. People learn by your assertive actions that you can be depended upon. They become confident that when necessary, you will take actions in a direct, open, candid and decisive manner.

You can develop and express assertiveness on a planned basis. You can make tough decisions on a step-by-step basis to develop more assertiveness and retain the flexibility necessary to win the confidence of the people you deal with. By starting with a number of easy or less important problems, you can practice being assertive until you feel comfortable with the larger, more difficult ones.

To develop more assertiveness, you need an overall framework in which to practice. Establish this framework by listing certain goals you wish to accomplish. These may be all-inclusive goals which cover business, social and family relationships. Each area, business, social and family group should include some easy, some intermediate and finally some very difficult goals.

After the goals have been established, pick one of the easier goals from each area and plan your approach to asserting yourself in relation to each goal. You may wish to use the R.A.P. system or "active listening" techniques as you deal with each person. For the purpose of practice, however, you will retain your assertive position. Your primary purpose in these practice sessions is to develop the ability to stick to your planned position You want the other person to agree with you on your position.

As you participate in each practice session, use the following rules as guidelines to insure your success:

1. Be assertive but polite; respect the rights, feelings, opinions and personal dignity of the other person.
2. Protect your own personal dignity. Do not let the other person ridicule or belittle your rights or feelings.
3. Listen carefully, express concern and tell the other person that you understand his position.
4. Demand agreement on the basis of your rights, the law or on moral principles

Many people who have taken formal "Assertiveness Training" courses have started their practice sessions with a list of twenty goals that they wish to accomplish. A popular first goal has involved a problem with a local grocery or department store. Most people have encountered resistance from store clerks and managers when trying to return an unsatisfactory item or when trying to get the store to order a brand that is preferred over the one the store has in stock.

How One Woman's Assertiveness Paid Off. One woman is reported to have demanded, as her first assertiveness practice session, that her local supermarket order and stock an item that she was currently driving to another part of town to purchase. She decided in advance that she would accept nothing less than an agreement, by the local store manager, to stock the product she desired. She correctly believed that the store's function was to provide the products she preferred. She made large weekly purchases at the store and decided that, if necessary, she would stop shopping at the store unless the manager ultimately agreed to her request.

The woman was assertive but polite in presenting her request to the store manager. She stated very clearly that she wanted the store manager to order and stock brand "X" as soon as possible. She explained that after purchasing her weekly grocery supplies at his store, she had been driving a considerable distance to get the one item and that she did not intend to do this any more.

The store manager explained the problem of trying to carry enough items to satisfy everyone and how they had selected the four most popular brands in order to please as many people as possible. The woman listened carefully and commented that their procedures seemed economical and generally effective. She asked if the manager agreed that the store should carry whatever items their customers wished to buy. When the manager concurred, she again repeated her request that brand "X" be stocked immediately so that she could discontinue her trips across town to purchase it.

The manager then indicated that he could not put a new item in just to please one person. The woman then asked the store manager if the writers of that policy intended for some people to be displeased. He quickly replied, "No." He said that their intentions were to provide substitute products that would please everyone. The woman then informed him that the substitute products did not please her. She wanted brand "X" and since the store policy was to please their customers, she would like to know when she would be able to find the product in the store.

The store manager explained that a "new item" request form would have to be filled out and it would then take about three weeks. The woman listened and expressed satisfaction with the procedure. She then asked if anything could happen to keep the product from being stocked once the request form was filled out. The manager said the request might be denied by the buyer. The woman then informed the store manager that she would bring a letter requesting the new item, that was to be attached to the request form.

She brought the letter back the same day. When she gave the letter to the manager, she asked that she be notified immediately if the request were turned down.

She told the store manager that she intended to go to the president of the company if her request were denied. She again reminded the store manager that she, as a steady customer, was entitled to service that was pleasing to her. She would not be pleased until the item she wanted to purchase was on the shelf.

The new item was approved, ordered and stocked. The woman who requested it was happy. She had been successful in her first attempt at being assertive and had eliminated the problem of traveling across town for one item. The store manager was also pleased because brand "X" surprised him and became one of his best-selling items.

11

How a Winning Reputation Gives You Psychological Leverage (Even Before You Speak the First Word)

People base what they say and the way they act upon what they expect from others. They alter their position, argue or try to please depending upon what they expect the consequences of their behavior to be. They will argue with those who they think will back down and act more passive toward those with whom they expect to argue. If you develop a winning reputation, people will be less likely to resist you simply because they expect you to win.

In this chapter, you learn to develop a winning reputation. You'll gain the Psychological Leverage that accompanies a winning reputation. You'll have the leverage of knowing the other person expects you to win even before you speak a word.

You will see, in this chapter, how to recognize situations that lead to adversity. You will be able to use these psychological techniques to protect and enhance your reputation. This chapter also covers speech techniques that promote a winning image and increase the Psychological Leverage of what you say.

HOW DEVELOPING A WINNING REPUTATION INCREASES YOUR PSYCHOLOGICAL LEVERAGE

You can develop a winning reputation by putting everything on the line in small gambles over points of minor importance. After you have shown consistently that you are willing to fight to the last straw over small things, your reputation will carry you. When a big challenge comes along, people will expect you to fight to the limit of your endurance. This is where your reputation comes in; you won't have to fight because people who do not wish to risk losing will not confront you at all. Your reputation will give you the Psychological Leverage to win even before you say anything.

THREE VISUAL IMAGES THAT HELP ESTABLISH A WINNING REPUTATION

Both your appearance and your actions affect the way other people see you. The quality of your dress as well as the way you act in public evoke mental images in people's minds. You can destroy an otherwise powerful image by dressing in a sloppy manner. You can lose the well-deserved reputation of a winner by acting in a way that appears cheap to others. The things you say and the way you say them add to or subtract from the image people hold of you. The following three guidelines will protect you against the errors that could have a negative impact on how people see you and at the same time provide a method for enhancing your image as a winner.

Tipping the Balance with Your Dress

You can tip the balance of your image to the favorable side by always buying the next bracket higher priced suit. Often an additional twenty or thirty dollars can mean the difference in a "run of the mill" image and a look of "class." Once you see the difference, all you have to do is ask yourself, "Which one makes me look like a winner?" Once you look, you'll know. All you have to do then is decide how much you are willing to pay to look like a winner.

Apply the same process to everything you buy. Remember that it only takes one weak link to break a chain. On the other hand, one extraordinary item can enhance the total picture. An exceptional tie, for example, can add class to a good suit. People are psychologically drawn to beautiful or exceptional quality. In the process of admiring an expensive tie, they concentrate less on the suit. The total package magnifies the image of what is inside, it adds balance to your image as a winner.

Tipping the Balance with Numbers

When people look at numbers they form psychological impressions of the value of numbers. They see a "one" as a single unit. Most often, they see two "ones" as two single units, not as a cumulative or doubled value. This only changes when you reach the number five. The "five" is seen as a significantly larger unit which is five times as large as a one. Psychologically a five dollar bill is seen as high value but four ones are seen as four units of low value.

The implication is clear. You can enhance your image, and your reputation, for example, by leaving a five dollar tip on those occasions where a three or four dollar tip would be acceptable. You can make the determination based upon the circumstances. There may be times, when the service is poor or you have made a small purchase, when a small tip is appropriate, but think carefully about the impression your tip will make. Will it be seen as a relatively high value or a relatively low value?

The Psychology of Silence

You probably know people who don't know when to keep quiet. Everyone has heard stories of the salesman who made the sale and then kept talking. He kept talking until he talked himself out of the sale. The more talking he did, the more the buyer realized the limitations of the salesman's product. The same thing applies in any conversation. If you only speak of those things you know something about, what you say will enhance your image and build your reputation.

If you try to fill the empty voids in conversation, your extraneous speech will expose weaknesses that create negative impressions in the minds of the people you talk to. You can develop a winning reputation by utilizing the psychology of silence. Just remain silent when you really have nothing to say.

I have found that salesmen generally talk too much. A friend of mine, who is a salesman, complained that he had a problem getting one of his customers to talk to him. He said he had tried everything. He had coaxed, pleaded, pressured and questioned all to no avail. He said the customer would not even answer his questions.

I knew my friend often talked so constantly that he left no time for me to make comments or to answer his questions. I suspected he was doing the same with his customer. After a lengthy description of all the things he had tried, he finally said, "What else can I do?" I suggested he try silence. I convinced him that a strategy of silence would cause the customer to say something to fill the void. I suggested that he ask a question occasionally to direct the conversation.

The salesman tried the strategy of silence and it worked. He later told me that his problem customer had become one of his best accounts. He was surprised, he said, to find out the customer previously felt that he had never been given a chance to tell the salesman his problems and what he really needed.

HOW TO SPEAK LIKE A WINNER

People tend to evaluate others by the quality of their speech. You can utilize speech techniques that will leave the impression of a strong and powerful person. These proven techniques will make you sound like a winner by improving the resonance and strength of your voice.

How Thinking Affects Your Speech

Your thoughts and feelings are reflected in your speech. Just as your emotions change the tone and volume of your voice, your thinking and feelings change the tone, pitch and volume of your voice. Think of the times you have heard someone speak in such a manner that his tone of voice showed disdain. Or, the time when you heard a mother talking to a baby in such a way that the baby smiled and cooed.

You can learn to express those warm tones in your voice by thinking about the feelings the mother has when she talks to a baby. You can enhance your image by speaking in a warm and friendly way. Lower your voice slightly, soften the tones and lower the rate of speed with which you speak and you will sound warm and friendly.

How Enthusiasm Helps Your Reputation

In all situations where you are trying to make a point, where you are trying to influence someone to accept your plan, be enthusiastic. To be enthusiastic, speak in positive terms. Act like a winner, add detail and color to show that you are enthusiastic and that you intend to be successful. Half of being successful is acting enthusiastic. As you act enthusiastic, get results and become successful, you begin to develop the reputation of a winner.

When you speak, you can develop enthusiasm by arousing interest. As you see others become interested, you will become more enthusiastic. One way to develop interest is to use pauses in your speech. The pause will create a delay in which others will have time to wonder what you are going to say next.

PROTECTING YOUR REPUTATION

You can protect your reputation as a "winner" by planning ahead. You can carefully plan your schedule to avoid situations that might result in a loss of prestige or power. You can be prepared to handle unexpected adversity by advance planning. By following certain guidelines that have been tested in marriage and family counselling sessions, you can control the situation and overcome adversity. Finally, there are a number of speech techniques, developed by psychologists and professional speakers that you can use to develop a winning reputation.

HOW TO AVOID SITUATIONS THAT CAN DAMAGE YOUR REPUTATION

If you are involved in group or organizational meetings, do everything in your power to avoid meetings scheduled at eleven in the morning. Meetings that are scheduled just before lunch may evoke aggressiveness that you do not normally encounter. This does not always happen, but as people become hungry they tend to become irritated more easily. The psychological effect of hunger is the same as for any deprived need. The person who feels deprived is frustrated and may become hostile.

The normal carryover effect of this hostility causes the person who is hungry to be more easily irritated and this irritation carries over into the discussion. It may cause an ordinarily calm person to engage in heated argument.

Other meetings to avoid are those that are called at a time when all members are fatigued. When everyone is tired, you can expect them to be easily irritated due to the frustration they feel. As people become more fatigued they become more easily frustrated and subject to anger. If you become involved in an argument due to someone's anger, your reputation may be damaged. So, the best strategy is to avoid discussion that seems to be leading into argument.

Some meetings are called for the primary purpose of praising the people who attend. Those meetings can help you, but a meeting called to chastise all the members can hurt your reputation. If you can avoid being publicly criticized, you will protect your reputation. Even though it is better to be criticized as part of a total group than on an individual basis, it is better not to be criticized at all.

A way to avoid harmful meetings is to make previous arrangements. If you know that a particular meeting is usually called at 11 A.M. on Tuesday, schedule something else for that time period that makes your attendance impossible. Do the same thing when you know a meeting is scheduled solely for the purpose of criticizing members. You may not be able to avoid all undesirable meetings, but you can avoid most of them.

I knew a product manager for a large beverage distributor who used this system to avoid meetings for years. He built the reputation of always being too busy to attend meetings. For years he was able to avoid the arguments that often ensued. When he was forced to attend a meeting, he always came in late. By coming late, he could later say that he missed any part of the meeting that he did not like.

HOW TO PREPARE FOR UNEXPECTED ADVERSITY

In spite of your best efforts to avoid unpleasant situations, there are times when you will be caught in them. There are meetings that people have to attend. There are situations that must be faced regardless of the hostility that may evolve.

Since adversity usually appears unexpectedly, you must prepare for the unexpected. You have an opportunity, when adversity arises, to use Psychological Leverage to enhance your reputation as a winner. The unexpected adversity usually appears in some form of anger. If you argue back and win the argument, you lose your reputation as an intelligent, logical and rational person. If the argument results in a stalemate or if you lose, you damage your reputation as a winner.

Using Psychological Leverage to Divert Unexpected Adversity

The way to use Psychological Leverage to enhance your reputation as a winner is to divert the conversation from the argument to something else. If you refuse to respond to a charge that you or someone under your direction erred in some way, you can't lose the argument. You can avoid the argument by diverting his attention to something else. The easiest and most readily available topic is his anger. You can do this with reflective statements.

To divert his attention, you simply say, "You seem very upset." You are now expressing concern for someone who was trying to attack you. You might, after he answers, say, "I'm concerned that this bothers you so much." You may use the R.A.P. system to further explore his problem. *This is using Psychological Leverage to divert the adversity back to the adversary, which enhances your winning reputation.*

Using Speech Techniques to Control Your Temper

Often unexpected adversity will be extremely harsh. Under harsh abuse, you may find it difficult to control your own temper. If you do not control your temper, you place yourself in the position of trying to win a shouting match. It can't be done. You not only are unable to make your point but you'll lose the reputation for being able to keep your cool.

Psychologists and other researchers have studied the voice and speech patterns of people who were engaged in argument or who displayed their temper. They were able to distinguish the differences between calm and angry speech from these studies. You can use this information to isolate the factors of angry speech and control them. You can concentrate, during times of irritation, on controlling your speech to give the impression of being calm. As you do this, the awareness of your attempts to appear calm will help you keep calm. The secret of controlling your temper through speech is to talk slowly and softly. If you do, you will appear cool and calm.

Using Your Personal Psychology to Control Your Temper

Another way to control your temper is to visualize a pleasant or sad scene. By forming a picture in your mind of a scene that you find relaxing, you will be able to ward off the feelings of frustration and anger. Psychological experiments have proven that anger can be reduced or eliminated simply by picturing a pleasant or sad scene. If you can think of some person or situation that you feel sympathy for, you can ward off anger by evoking this sympathetic feeling. It is not possible to simultaneously feel sympathetic and angry. Nor is it possible to feel the joy of a pleasant scene and anger at the same time.

You can utilize these personal psychological techniques at once. Perhaps you have some vacation spot or other place that is especially relaxing to you. Practice bringing this picture into your mind. Think of the overall scene and try to recapture the feeling you have when you are there. If you have a problem bringing the whole picture into memory, think of the individual parts that make up the whole.

If you don't have a place that you can picture from memory, cut a picture out of a magazine of a lake, forest, snow capped mountain, or anything that you find relaxing. Carry this picture around with you and look at it over and over until you have every detail memorized. Soon you will be able to relax simply by forming the picture in your mind.

How a West Coast Salesman Developed Psychological Leverage in Dealing with His Customers. One of the salesmen who attended a seminar with me told me how he had applied the new techniques of active listening and how he had developed a winning reputation. The salesman had recently been assigned a new territory and was not doing well. The customers on his route had not bought from his company in the past so he had to prove his products as well as himself.

The salesman decided that his only chance was to build a reputation as a winner. Since he had been successful on his previous territory, he had many success stories to tell. He wove these success stories into each presentation to show the customers that he was confident about his products. When he was unable to make a sale, he acted surprised but gave no indication that one sale was important to him.

When he did make a sale, he followed up on every aspect of the transaction to make sure the sale was successful. He made sure the product was delivered on time, was displayed properly and that advertising material was available to support the sale. He prepared special signs and displays and often came into the stores and prepared samples to give shoppers. His sales were successful because he made them successful.

He bought a tape recorder and practiced his sales presentations. He practiced voice techniques that sounded warm and friendly. But he also practiced being forceful and determined. He imagined that his customers would become unexpectedly angry and then he would practice diverting the conversation to the customers feelings rather than the point the customer was angry about. He learned to control his temper and he rapidly developed a reputation as a very level headed salesman. Just as the concern he showed the customer gave him a favorable image, so did his following up on a sale earn him a reputation as a winner. His sales were always successful and his customers learned to expect them to be successful.

TWO WAYS TO CONFRONT CRITICS

Differences of opinion often cause controversy. The intellectual basis of these differences is due to the different background of each individual. Each person's values, tastes and desires lead to experiences that expose a unique set of facts. The person whose values, tastes and desires are different from yours, naturally encounters different experiences than you do. He seeks different experiences and this may lead to extremely diverse facts which are unique to that person.

The controversy that evolves out of the differences of opinion is best dealt with by using the R.A.P. system. There are some people, however, who criticize or heckle not because of a different opinion but from their desire to belittle you, enhance their own ego or to have fun at your expense. A different strategy is often helpful in dealing with these people.

How to Use "Psychological Leverage" to Neutralize Criticism

One way to neutralize criticism is to simply agree with the "heckler" that, under certain conditions, he may be right. You can expand on this point and take the wind out of the heckler's sails. By using a few minutes to agree that there may be some application for his idea, you can then go on with your topic. Since you didn't argue with him there is no reason to ask him for further clarification. You have psychologically disarmed him and you look good in the eyes of everyone else in the group.

You always enhance your own image by being courteous to hecklers. You can show courtesy to hecklers or critics by talking politely and by smiling and acting friendly and by thanking them for their comments. You can show respect, appreciation and courtesy to a heckler and never show that you are irritated by his undue criticism. You might comment that you appreciate examining other ideas. You might say, "It's good to introduce new ideas so that we have alternatives to compare." Then ask someone else for a comparison, thank him and move on.

Sometimes a heckler will keep heckling no matter what you say. When he begins to interfere and keeps you from finishing or is taking too much time, ask him to be a nice guy and wait until you have explained your position. You might say, "Once I have presented the facts and everyone understands what I'm trying to say, we will be able to understand your point better." Often you can silence a persistent heckler by telling him, "Our private conversation is keeping the group from understanding today's topic. Why don't you and I wait until the meeting is over and discuss your remaining points privately. That way we won't have to bore the rest of the group."

How to Use Psychological Leverage to Eliminate Criticism

If you are a member of some organization, you can eliminate criticism by tying your idea to some organizational policy or goal. Then anyone who attacks you is attacking the organization. This is not likely to happen. If it does, just sit back, listen and let him "hang" himself.

Act assertively when dealing with criticism but don't blind yourself to reason. It is possible that you could be wrong or that the critic may have a good point. Also, no matter how right you are, you will not always be able to sell your ideas. Keep an open mind, be willing to listen and compare other ideas and then present your evidence forcefully. Remember that listening and trying to understand the other person builds an obligation for the other person to listen to you.

TEN POINTS THAT HELP ELIMINATE CRITICISM

The following ten points are based on psychological and educational research and have been tested in everyday situations in business. They have been found to be effective in stopping unfounded criticism and in gaining understanding.

1. Keep cool, don't become angry.
2. Listen first, avoid judging, evaluating or approving the points made by the critic.
3. Put the other person at ease, be empathetic and show concern for his feelings.
4. Show that you want to hear his ideas and are listening by summarizing his points.
5. Be patient, give him the necessary time to finish.
6. Give him some degree of credit by suggesting that some part of his idea will work or that under certain conditions, his idea may work.
7. Ask him to listen to your evidence to see if it relates to his point.
8. Develop a neutral framework so that he can accept your idea without having to admit that he is wrong.
9. Present examples from his background that your ideas could be applied to.
10. Present your final argument very forcefully, show that you are confident of the merit of your proposal.

How a Product Marketing Manager Neutralized a Critic. At a weekly marketing meeting, Harry, one of the product marketing managers, began criticizing his fellow managers for errors in their daily inventory records. Harry managed a low volume product line and seldom had errors in his own inventory. The other product managers had daily production added to their inventory from both a day and a night production shift. They also had shipments made from the inventory twice daily. Harry had twice daily shipments from his stock also but he only had additions to his inventory once a week.

Harry took the product managers to task, one by one. He had a list of differences between actual and reported inventory as of the morning of the meeting. Harry also had developed a list of problems each inventory error had caused. He pointed out that money was being lost and the product managers were not doing their jobs. The managers being criticized were surprised at the attack. They either responded by making excuses or said nothing. When Harry turned on Bill, the product manager with the highest volume department, he found that Bill was prepared for unexpected adversity. Bill asked Harry if Harry had worked out any plan to eliminate the problem.

Harry was now the surprised one. Not only did Harry not have a plan, he was now on the defensive. Harry said he was only trying to point out the mistakes that had been made so the department managers could correct their own mistakes. Bill stated that everyone would like to correct the problem and asked Harry if he had made a list of any of the reasons for the errors. Bill wanted to know if the cause was primarily associated with new production or with shipments.

Harry snapped that it was not his job to run their "damn' departments for them. "Harry," he said, "you seem to be really upset and concerned about our inventory errors. I understand just how you feel. Why don't you tell us just how big a problem the errors are causing." Harry replied, "The problem is that you people are not keeping your inventory records properly." Bill retorted, "Harry, I'm trying to solve a problem that you brought up. I've listened to you and I understand your concern. You brought it to our attention and now we're trying to solve it. You don't seem to be trying to help. What are you trying to do?" Harry was now on the defensive again. It was perfectly clear to everyone that Bill had turned the tables on Harry. Harry said, "I was just trying to point out some areas that need improvement."

Bill continued, "You seem to have extra time each day, Harry; perhaps you could put some time into determining how and where the mistakes are being made. This way you will be helping us even more." Harry said that he didn't have time every day, but Bill was not ready to let him off the hook. Bill very forcefully stated that Harry obviously had some time available. After all, he had found time to make the list of errors.

Bill concluded the conversation by saying, "Harry, you get a list of the possible causes of these problems and we will help you do the job that you say you would like to see done. We'll help you solve the problems with the inventory." Harry mumbled something about doing it when he found time and the discussion was closed.

Bill enhanced his reputation as a winner without directly attacking or belittling Harry. But everyone knew that Bill had won. Bill had turned the criticism back on Harry. If Harry had time to check on the errors that the other department managers had made, then he had time to look for the source of the problems. Harry talked himself into additional responsibility. Bill used Psychological Leverage to gain Harry's acceptance of that responsibility.

12 ———

How to Use Psychological Power to Get Things Done

There are two basic forms of power. One is organizational power that accompanies positions of authority within an organization. This power is relative to the hierarchal position in the organization and is also called "positional power."

Organizational power is derived from a philosophical base. The principles of "justice for all," "cooperation for the common good," "teaching religious ideals" and "efficiency of specialization" are a few of the many influences that resulted in the formation of organizations.

The second basic power form, which has unlimited application, is personal power. Personal power grows out of a psychological base. In this chapter, we will cover the use of psychology-based personal power and how it can be used to get things done. You will be given techniques that will help you utilize your own abilities and the power of other people to multiply your own power. This chapter reveals the secrets of how great leaders develop their power. You can use these techniques to develop Psychological Leverage which will help you get what you want done.

FOUR CHARACTERISTICS OF PERSONAL POWER

There are four basic characteristics of personal power. Many people have gained power from utilizing only one or two of them. If you learn and utilize practical psychological techniques, you can double the power of what you say. By developing all four characteristics, you will be able to get more done. You will also find that it is

167

easier to get things done because these techniques apply to the psychology of the other person. They create a desire for the other person to do what you want done. The personal power techniques are:

1. The ability to persuade others to do something you want done.
2. The ability to use the power of other people to multiply your own.
3. The ability to allocate rewards to those who comply with your directions.
4. The willingness to place justice and truth above personal desire.

The Ability to Persuade Others to Do Something You Want Done

The science of persuasion is the analysis of the values, wants, needs and expectations of people and the systematic development of a synthesizing link between what you want and one of those values, wants, needs or expectations. To get another person to do what you want done, the other person must feel comfortable with your idea. He needs to bathe your idea in his own thoughts. He needs to dry it with the towels of his past experience. He needs to clothe it with his own ideals, beliefs and value system. The following steps will help you accomplish this goal:

1. Analyze the statements made by the other person to determine his motivations, values and expectations.
2. Listen carefully to what the other person says; express empathy for his views. This builds an obligation for him to listen to you.
3. Express your ideas in terms that help satisfy the needs the other person is already motivated to fulfill.
4. Express your ideas in terms that match the self-image indicated by the other person's values and expectations.
5. Use some of the words of the other person to make the idea comfortable for him.
6. Ask the other person to comment on how your idea might work in some of the areas he is involved in.
7. Compare your idea with some other idea and ask him to evaluate it.
8. Demonstrate how the idea will help him accomplish some goal.
9. Expound your point of view in a self-confident and assertive way.

The Ability to Use the Power of Other People to Multiply Your Own

Real power comes from the accumulation of the power of a number of people. The voice that cries for freedom from the darkened cell or the deserted street, for example, is the voice of a powerless man. But the voice of the man that speaks from the throng, the voice that speaks for and from the multitude is the voice of a powerful man.

The secret of all the great leaders of society is that they assumed the power of the multitude. Power moves *from* the crowd *to* the speaker who speaks for the ideals and needs of the group. The speaker's power is multiplied in proportion to the size of the crowd. The following points will help you multiply your power:

1. Speak on the behalf of a group and the group will support your goals.
2. Express your ideas in terms of the group's goals.
3. Make some personal sacrifice for the greater good of the group.
4. Develop a "great idea" that expresses the values of the group.
5. Be persistent in the pursuit of the group's goals.

The Ability to Allocate Rewards to Those Who Comply with Your Directions

People who hold organizational power are inherently provided, by the organization, monetary and authority resources that may be allocated to those who comply with the directions from above. These resources are limited and are not appealing to all people. There are other rewards, however, that gratify the psychological needs of people that are unlimited. The use of these rewards forms the basis of psychological personal power.

By using the technique of satisfying the psychological needs of others, you multiply your personal power. The following guideline provides a method that may be used in rewarding others to double your Psychological Power.

1. Reward others by giving them some degree of freedom. You can do this in conversation by remaining silent long enough for them to completely express their thoughts and opinions.

2. Offer the reward of support and encouragement. Rather than criticize someone for an error, relate to the progress that has been made.

3. Provide prestige and respect through verbal summaries and questions. A summary shows that you hold the other party high enough in esteem to want to make sure that you understand what he says. Obviously you must feel his thoughts important or you would not care enough to try to remember or understand them. By using questions and summary statements, you provide a reward that satisfies the individual's need for esteem.

4. Promote participation. By allowing others to participate with you in planning or evaluating the activities under your control you satisfy the need for learning, growth and socialization. These rewards will help you get things done with commitment on the part of the other person.

The Willingness to Place Justice and Truth Above Personal Desire

To acquire the added power that accrues from the support of other people, you must win the trust of those people. Trust evolves from a belief that you are truthful and that you practice justice on a completely impartial basis. If a few get special justice, then trust is lost.

The following actions will help you acquire the support and trust of the people you deal with. By placing justice and truth above personal desire, you will be able to retain the power of the group.

1. Confront adversity. The willingness to stand up and proclaim your stand against adversity will win you the respect and admiration of the group you represent. Whenever someone expounds a point of view that is counter to the view of your group or counter to the view you hold, speak up. Make it known that you disagree. Do not express your differences in a hostile way. You can win more respect and trust by speaking in a quiet intellectual way. People respect quiet, calm opposition but not argumentative or hostile opposition.

2. Resist the unjust. There is as much power in resistance as there is in confrontation. In a way resistance is confrontation. The resister is saying, "I refuse to comply with an unjust or unethical request."

3. Use the power of speech techniques to uphold the ideals of the group. Most people will be attracted to the support of a person who will speak up for group ideals. You can use speech techniques to pursue the goals of the group. If you persistently pursue group goals, your power will evolve into a quiet but commanding force. Remember, real power is quiet, smooth and all pervasive. Like water moving through a pipe, it moves everything in its path.

4. Be positive in your approach. The more submissive person seeks leaders who are assertive and positive. They seek a source of strength to lean on. They will support you in order to receive the feeling of security they derive from your strength.

A Salesman Who Had More Psychological Power Than His Boss. Glen Wilson, after transferring from an Eastern territory, had built his sales territory up to $25,000 per week gross sales in three months. Glen was just beginning to feel good about his progress when he received a note from his sales manager, George Dillings. George directed Glen to attend a three day workshop, with his fellow salesmen, to find ways to improve what George described as unacceptable sales results.

Glen knew morale was low among the salesmen due to George's pressure for increasing sales. Glen thought the workshop was a good idea as it might help clear the air among the salesmen and improve morale.

George opened the workshop by directing the men to find a way to increase sales by thirty per cent. George was a hard driving sales manager who continually pushed even his best men past the point of endurance. Part of his current sales problem was caused by this behavior. Two of his best men had become fed up and quit. George was now increasing the pressure on the remaining salesmen to make up for the sales lost when the two men quit. George's final remark was, "I don't know how you are going to do it, but it has to be done. Work it out in this workshop, and then get out there and get it done."

Glen's knowledge that morale was low was just the "tip of the iceberg." The men were completely demoralized. As soon as George left the room, Phil, a twenty-year veteran salesman, said, "Did you hear that last remark? There is absolutely no justice here. He wants us to share the two vacated territories and I'm already driving two hundred and fifty miles a day. How does he think we can make any sales calls when we spend all day driving?"

Glen listened and analyzed the remarks of the other salesmen. There were many gripes but the one thing that came through from everyone was the fact that they had to drive too many miles each day. Glen suggested they work out a plan to rearrange the territories including the hiring of new salesmen and reducing the mileage to a manageable level for the best sales results. Two people answered together, "He won't do anything we recommend. When this is over, he'll just tell us to get out and get the job done. That's his answer for everything."

Glen remarked that he felt the situation should be confronted.

He suggested they work out a plan and then he would personally confront George with the plan. When the plan was complete, Glen took it to George.

George was surprised that they had really worked out a plan. He said, "They usually wind up by asking for more promotions." Glen explained that the plan required two men to be transferred in order to reduce their driving time. There were seven territory changes and at least two replacements were needed to cover the territories vacated by the resignations. An additional man would have to be hired to cover the area that could not be efficiently covered by the new system. Glen suggested the possibility that the new area could be handled by phone from the office, since they were all small accounts.

George did accept the plan. He had not been able to get anything constructive out of the salesmen before. His pressure tactics had led to low morale and frequent resignations. Glen's approach was to persuade the salesmen to prepare a plan which would reflect the needs of the whole group. By pushing the truth and confronting the sales manager, Glen was able to get the job done. Glen, in the process, built a rapport with the salesmen that gave him support and power in future dealings with the sales manager.

TWO WAYS TO BUILD YOUR PERSONAL POWER

You can build your own personal power by establishing a psychological power base and by using speech techniques that project power. There are six specific actions that you can take to establish a psychological power base and there are five techniques that you can use to project power when you speak.

You can rapidly develop the ability to project power by concentrating on the five speech techniques. The more time you devote to practice, the more rapidly you will gain proficiency. The establishment of real psychological power, however, will come more slowly.

The multiplication of your personal power through gaining group support requires time. You must allow time for the group members to become confident in you. You must demonstrate the pursuit of ideals and goals that are held by the group. You must also demonstrate that you are worthy of the group's trust and that you possess the individual characteristics that the group admires.

1. ESTABLISHING YOUR PSYCHOLOGICAL POWER BASE

The following six steps will guide you in establishing your power base. These steps will strengthen your individual characteristics of integrity and assertiveness and will gain you the support of the group you are dealing with. The six steps are:

1. Stand on integrity, avoid compromise.
2. Define your goals in terms of high moral principles.
3. Confront every obstacle that interferes with your goals.
4. Join compatible groups to gain numerical support for your ideas.
5. Protect and support the members of your group.
6. Promote justice through the equal treatment of all people.

Stand on Integrity

When you are trying to promote an idea or argument, you will invariably run into resistance. Someone will want you to change or alter your idea or compromise your arguments. You can prepare to overcome these resistances by developing your arguments on the basis of honesty and integrity. Build honesty and integrity directly into your idea, proposal or request and you will have a built in defense. No one can expect you to compromise honesty, integrity or high moral values.

Define Your Goals in Terms of High Moral Principles

Just as it is difficult to attack integrity, it is difficult to attack moral principles. A little thought in preparation may reveal a high moral principal that you can relate your argument to. By relating your arguments and ideas to honesty, integrity and high moral values, you develop the "Psychological Power" that enables you to refuse to compromise.

Confront Obstacles That Interfere with Your Goals

Many people miss the opportunity to enhance their power when they avoid confronting the many daily obstacles that irritate or cause them problems. Confront, rather than worry about, every situation that irritates you and soon you will be leading a more relaxed life and your reputation as an assertive, powerful person will continue to grow.

I know a successful woman, who as a teen-ager was a shy and retiring high school graduate who suffered continually because of her inability to talk to people. She missed the joy of laughing and socializing with people and felt more dejected and depressed each day.

Each day she told herself, "Today I will change. Today I will force myself to talk and make friends." But each day she gave in to her fear and backed away from her opportunities to socialize. She realized that she was losing the battle and decided to take drastic action.

She began searching for a job as a receptionist. She persisted in her search until, finally, she was successful. She became a receptionist and slowly became comfortable in conversation. She confronted her problem and won. She is no longer shy and reserved. Today she is a successful talk show hostess on a local radio station in her home town.

Join Compatible Groups

Groups that have compatible ideas will support you, if they know about you. Find these groups and join them. This also gives you a sounding board for your ideas. The group members will discuss and help you find ways to sell your ideas if they agree with them. The power of the group is then added to your personal power. As you promote the goals of the group, by winning their support, you increase your Psychological Power.

Protect and Support the Members of Your Group

All successful leaders know they must support the group that gives them their power. You may at times have to make small sacrifices for the good of the group. When you do, make sure the group members know about it. The knowledge of your personal efforts to protect or improve the group will enhance your standing in the group and solidify your power.

Promote Justice Through the Equal Treatment of All People

The concept of equal justice for all has been carried over from law into everyday life. Everyone expects to be treated equally. No favors or special privileges can be given to one without being given equally to everyone in the group.

2. USING VOICE TECHNIQUES THAT PROJECT POWER

Your voice is like a musical instrument that can be used to dramatize what you say. You can emphasize important words by timing, inflection, volume changes or tone changes. You can develop more power by altering the sounds of your voice to sound more powerful. You can, through practice, learn to speak in such a way that you will project an image of power through your speech.

Sounding Assertive

You can sound assertive simply by slightly raising your voice and placing emphasis on the last word of a sentence. You might say, "I'm not going to put up with his inefficiency any longer." You would raise your voice slightly as you begin the sentence, raise the volume more on the word "inefficiency" and emphasize the last word, "longer." Be cautious that you don't sound too assertive. If you become overly loud, you will sound hostile rather than assertive.

Showing Interest in Other People

You can accumulate and hold the power that is derived from the numerical support of other people by showing interest in them. To show interest in others, watch your method of speech. If you speak too rapidly, too softly or too loudly, you are showing a lack of concern for the other person. To show concern and interest in the other person, adjust your speech to what is comfortable for him.

You can determine what is comfortable to the other person by starting with a normal rate of speech and moderate volume. If the other person asks you to repeat your words, you may not be speaking loudly enough. So, raise your voice and see if that eliminates the problem. If he continues to ask you to repeat, then talk more slowly or pause more between sentences. Using pauses after you give each point is courteous and shows interest in the other person. It also gives him an opportunity to respond.

Sounding Trustworthy

You can develop speaking methods that give your voice the sound of trustworthiness. If you speak in a friendly and relaxed way, you will sound pleasing and trustworthy. If you smile and act friendly, your voice will automatically take on a pleasing quality. Low tones are generally considered to sound more trustworthy than high tones. You should vary the rate and range of your speech, however, to add variety and interest to what you say.

Showing Enthusiasm

You can show enthusiasm in your voice by using variations in your pitch and inflection. You can develop this ability to change the sounds of your voice through practice. Think of yourself as being an enthusiastic person and then make an effort to sound enthusiastic as you talk. You will very quickly form the habit of varying the pitch and inflection of your speech which will give you a naturally enthusiastic sound.

The enthusiasm you show will incite enthusiasm in others and increase your power in getting things done. Often you can evoke enthusiasm from other people by mild encouragement or by reminding them of the consequences of an indifferent approach to their task.

One group that was encouraged to overcome an indifferent attitude had been working tirelessly trying to reach agreement on an important document. Unable to reach agreement, they finally became so disillusioned that they indifferently began to put together a compromise that no one really believed in.

At that point, their chairman offered these brief comments, "If we offer to the people something of which we ourselves do not approve, how can we, afterwards, defend our work? Let us raise a standard to which the wise and the honest may gladly repair. The event is in the hands of God."

The document gives evidence to the power of General George Washington's words of encouragement. The group he addressed, the delegates to the Constitutional Convention in Philadelphia in 1789, worked with new vigor and produced the Constitution of the United States.

Developing Power in Your Voice

Adding power to the sound of your voice can be accomplished by developing good speaking habits such as the ones we have just covered. You need, however, to add forcefulness and intensity to your speech to project a total image of power.

Place your hand on your chest, draw in a deep breath and press against your chest as you speak. You will feel the power of your breath against your chest. This shows you that you have the power to increase the forcefulness of your speech. Think about this power and think of speaking forcefully. The realization that you have the power and the determination to use it will insure your success.

To develop the forcefulness you need, you must practice intensifying the sounds you make. You can best accomplish this by using a tape recorder. Make a recording of a two or three minute talk and think about making a powerful impression as you speak. Purposely sound some words louder than others so that you can hear the difference.

Play the recording back and listen carefully to determine how forceful and powerful you sound. As you listen, write down any part of the talk that doesn't sound forceful so that you can add emphasis to that portion on the next recording. Keep recording and playing back until you can hear the forcefulness and power coming through.

How a Branch Manager Used His Psychological Power to Win Support. Carl Beckley, a midwestern manufacturing branch manager, used his personal Psychological Power to resolve an argument and won support from two management subordinates. As Carl walked through the plant, Tom, a product marketing manager, stopped him. Tom asked, "Will you tell John to change tonight's production schedule? I can't get him to understand that I have to fill tonight's orders." Carl responded, "Why don't you both tell me your individual problems and maybe we can find a solution that will do the most good for everyone. We want to increase our profits but we also want to keep problems to a minimum." Carl's remarks were a reminder of a high moral value that the group was committed to and also a reminder that he would protect each individual's interests.

Carl asked, "Tom, how important is it to you to change the production schedule after John has already set it up?" Tom replied, "I need products that he has not scheduled to fill my customer's needs." Carl continued, "Is there any more to it than that?" As Tom answered, Carl listened and analyzed what Tom said in order to determine what his feelings, motivations and values were. As Carl listened, he found that Tom really wanted the authority to change production without going to John at all. Tom felt production scheduling was his responsibility.

Carl next talked to John and found that John felt that he must keep responsibility for scheduling due to his responsibility for controlling the time of the men on the production line. Carl supported both men in their reasoning and in their goals. Carl successfully convinced each of the men that his primary goal was to find a solution that was the most profitable and cause the least problems for each man. Eventually he found the solution.

Carl proposed that Tom schedule the products that were to be produced each night, but John would control the actual assignment of the men and set the men's working schedule. Carl was able to use some of the words and ideas of both men in presenting the solution. Both men accepted the idea and began to work better together and became more supportive of Carl's ideas on other matters.

13

How Using Psychological Leverage Gets Results in Group Meetings

You can get outstanding results from group members by developing a feeling of high morale. If the individual members feel that their group is an elite group, they will be motivated to be more productive. Each time the group makes a creative contribution by solving a problem or developing new ideas, the feeling of being an elite group is reinforced and morale is increased.

Many studies in business have confirmed that high productivity results from the development of high morale. Time after time, studies that compared supervisory methods with results achieved, revealed that supervisors who created conditions leading to high morale had the highest production records. These results were verified in all types of group activity. Production, engineering, accounting, marketing and management groups all performed better when their morale was high.

In this chapter you will see how you can develop high morale. You will learn guidelines for keeping control of the group discussion, developing new ideas from negative viewpoints and how to recognize and neutralize productivity barriers.

SIX CHARACTERISTICS OF HIGH MORALE

There are six basic characteristics that were found to exist in the highest producing of the groups that were studied by the university research teams. The six characteristics were:

1. The group members held a high standard of excellence.

2. Each individual received personal satisfaction through group participation.
3. The group supervisors supported individual group members.
4. Group members developed self-confidence due to feedback provided by their supervisors.
5. Group supervisors acted as advisors and helpers to group members.
6. The supervisors promoted an "elite group" feeling among the group members.

You can provide the guidance and support necessary to establish these six characteristics within your group. By developing high morale, you will get better participation and higher productivity.

1. DEVELOPING A HIGH STANDARD OF EXCELLENCE

You can use group psychology to raise the group's standard of excellence. Group members who hold high standards of excellence impose their standards on other members. You can raise the standards of the whole group by raising the standards of two or three influential members. Research has shown that group members will tend to imitate influential members in their activities and attitudes.

Blending Group and Individual Psychology to Establish Goals

You can encourage the development of a high standard of excellence by establishing high goals. Let the group know that you expect great things from them. Psychologists have found that the greater the expectations of the group leader, the higher will be the performance of the group. You can blend group and individual psychology to achieve high group performance. You can establish high goals for the group and realistic goals for each group member to accomplish your objectives.

Using the Psychology of the Other Person to Improve Performance

Each group member must be given goals that are achievable but that are difficult enough to cause him to stretch and grow in order to achieve them. By assigning tough but attainable goals, you are tying in to the psychology of each person. Each person's own psychological motivations will guide him to higher performance if he is encouraged to study, research and give strenuous thought to his project. These motivations can be brought into play by letting each person partici-pate in developing the plan or strategy to reach those goals.

Phil Everton, a high school basketball coach in a small eastern town, was concerned with the lack of commitment by the players. Often they missed practice and rarely showed any enthusiasm when they did practice. The team had only won two games in the last three years. Phil knew that a win against a strong team would create en-thusiasm among the fans and lead to future support for the team.

Phil selected a game with a team they had never beaten and called the team together to discuss his plan. He explained that he wanted to develop new plays and perfect them prior to that game. He then asked the team members to work up playing diagrams for any ideas they might have for new plays.

As the team members became involved in developing new plays, they became committed to winning what had now become known as the "big game." Everyone showed up for practice daily and began to win with their regular plays, holding their new "secret" plays for the "big game."

By the time the "big game" came, everyone in town was talking about the local team's winning streak. Speculation ran high about the local team's chances in the "big game." A week before the game, Phil gave the local paper just enough information to create interest. He simply said the team had a surprise play for the "big game."

The local team had practiced the new plays until they were perfected, but did not use them during the first half of the game. They held the visiting team to a tied score at the end of the first half. In the second half they started using their new plays. They took a quick lead and continually increased the lead until they won the game by twenty points.

Phil used the psychology of the team members to build the team. Their own motivation to succeed with their own ideas led to the commitment to practice which led to winning the game.

2. PROVIDING SATISFACTION THROUGH PARTICIPATION

You can provide a wide variety of personal satisfactions to each group member by permitting each to participate in discussions of his goals and the procedures to be used for attaining them. The prestige and recognition that each member feels from having his ideas or suggestions listened to, provides the motivation for maximum indi-vidual effort. The social rewards of affiliation with a prestigious group reinforce individual initiative and create a desire to remain a group member.

You can control the feeling of the group by making sure no one feels a failure. If an idea is presented that seems unworkable or too costly to put into effect, you can suggest it be tested and written up in a report. The writer may discover for himself that the idea is unworkable and will be spared the feeling of failure that might otherwise occur. You might establish a standard procedure whereby all ideas and suggestions must be approved by a screening committee before they are put into effect. The screening committee can reject the proposal without affecting the person's prestige. Each member enjoys the immediate prestige, recognition and affiliation of group participation but does not have to face feelings of rejection when his ideas are not feasible.

3. SUPPORTING INDIVIDUAL EFFORTS TO GROW

Each group member is challenged by group norms to grow and improve. He is motivated to retain his place in the group by sharpening his skills, learning new techniques and improving his individual performance. You can develop Psychological Leverage, with anyone, by supporting his attempts to meet the requirements of the group.

You can help this person through his early efforts to improve. As a person tries new methods or stretches toward new levels of proficiency, he often encounters failure. Your supportive role, at this time, is crucial to his success. You can encourage him by pointing out that you expect some problems and errors since the primary way we learn is through error. If he feels comfortable in making errors, he will continue to try to learn the new techniques and skills involved.

4. PROVIDING FEEDBACK TO BUILD CONFIDENCE

You can keep the group on a progressive course by providing feedback on their progress before errors become habitual. You can reinforce their correct actions the same way. Early feedback will reinforce their correct activities and encourage further improvement. This positive feedback will also help build confidence. As a person develops confidence, he becomes more vigorous in performing the correct actions. If he receives positive feedback from the more vigorous actions, he feels even more confident.

Confidence building, however, is a tricky matter. Confidence can't be built just by telling someone he is great. There must be clear evidence to support the ascribed level of competency. People must determine their own level of competency and they do so through their own reasoning as well as from feedback from others. You can help a person develop self-confidence by showing him his actual results. Show him records and let him compare his results against his own previous results and the previous results of others.

Concentrate on Positive Aspects When Correcting Errors

The same reasoning applies to correcting errors as to building self-confidence. The individual should be able to see the error for himself. You can point out specific errors by relating them to specific results. But remember not to refer to the errors as a personal failure. Refer to them as part of the learning process. Concentrate on the positive aspects. Point out that some learning occurred from making the error and how a slight change can result in increased productivity. If progress has been made, point it out and encourage further trials.

5. ACTING AS AN ADVISOR AND HELPER

Let your group members know that you are there to advise and help them. Many people refrain from asking for help or advice because they fear criticism. They feel they'll be thought incapable or unknowledgeable if they ask for help in carrying out their assigned task.

You can overcome this problem by showing them they have nothing to fear. Let them know that you realize they are trying to improve productivity and that their desire to improve naturally leads them to seek other people's advice and opinions. If you show the group members that your intentions are to advise and help rather than to criticize, they will come to you for help when they need it. The advice and help you provide will help them avoid many errors and will give you the Psychological Leverage to guide their efforts and improve productivity.

Researchers at the University of Michigan studied twenty-four separate groups of supervisors and their workers to determine the effect the behavior and attitude of supervisors had on their subordinates. The conclusions of this study indicated that the supervisors who acted as advisors and helpers to their subordinates got substantially better production than supervisors who did not act in that way.

The employees of the helpful supervisors became very productive individually and as a group. They seemed to be happy in the pursuit of their job goals. They cheerfully completed their tasks without wasting time. The help and advice of their supervisors gave them confidence and a feeling of dignity in performing their job.

6. BUILDING AN ELITE GROUP

You can use Psychological Leverage to raise group performance far above most expectations. By relating to the psychology of a person's desire to be a member of an elite group, you can encourage greater group productivity. By providing freedom for group interaction through discussion or group activities, you build a climate from which highly productive group norms evolve.

You can influence those norms by providing group members with information on the goals of the organization and by providing feedback on the group results. To hold an image of an elite group, they must have some feedback to support their feelings. They must feel that as a group they know more, are better trained and earn more than the industry average.

By offering training programs to help the individual members, you improve productivity and again reap double benefits. When their productivity warrants it, increase their rewards above normal standards. As they become aware that they are more productive and are receiving better than average rewards, they will become even more productive due to the reinforcement of the "elite group" feeling.

FOUR PARTICIPATION TECHNIQUES THAT INSURE SUCCESS

Once you have a plan in action for developing an elite group with high morale, you can begin to work on the factors that will make the group more productive. The development of high morale will give you a committed, creative group, but that group will still need guidance, stimulation, support and challenge to maximize productivity. The following four activities will help develop a highly productive group.

1. A FIVE-POINT GUIDE TO KEEP THE DISCUSSION ON THE PROBLEM

Any time that a group of people are drawn together to solve a problem or discuss an action, there will be some extraneous discussion due to the varied and complex psychological needs that all

humans have. The gathering provides an opportunity for the fulfillment of the often subconscious needs for prestige, recognition, independence, security and socialization through conversation in the
group. Without controls, this motivation to fulfill psychological
needs will divert the group from the goal or problem they are assem-
bled to discuss. The following five points will keep the group on the
problem and at the same time fulfill their individual psychological
needs:

1. Define the problem in terms that mesh with the needs of the
group.

2. Point out that there is a difference between current conditions
and the goal or solution you wish to achieve. The difference or "gap"
provides the challenge and means for self-development. The group
can fulfill their prestige needs and the individual can fulfill his need
for recognition by "filling the gap."

3. Set a time limit and appoint a Time Advisor to notify the
group when extraneous conversation is eating up needed time.

4. Provide frequent "breaks" so the group members can fulfill,
through informal conversation, those personal needs they are unable
to fulfill during the more formal discussion period. During the more
formal portion of the meeting, only one person can talk at a time.
During the "break" up to fifty per cent of the group can talk at the
same time. The buildup of emotions or pressure to fulfill personal
psychological needs is reduced during this conversational "break."

5. Point out that the group is responsible for finding a solution.
The feeling of being part of an elite group will act as a stimulus to the
members to find a group solution.

2. FOUR STEPS IN TURNING NEGATIVE VIEWPOINTS TO YOUR ADVANTAGE

Every idea, every suggestion, every thought expressed in a meeting will be seen as unworkable by some people. One person may not
think the approach is correct, another might think the wrong problem
is being worked on. Another may think you are attacking too large a
problem or may simply think the wrong people are working on the
problem. Every negative remark that is made in a meeting is a result of
a different perspective on the problem.

You can utilize negative viewpoints to bring out additional
knowledge from the group that may result in a better solution. If one
member says, "We can't solve this problem" it may mean that he
thinks an additional source of knowledge is needed. Upon question-

ing, it might turn out that he sees a large part of the problem requiring an analysis by an accountant, engineer or some other specialist who is not in attendance.

The importance of drawing out the reason for the negative view, is that you might overlook an important element of the problem if you ignore the negative remark. The greatest sales contest design will have no value if there is no way to account for each salesman's results. This problem might be exposed through drawing out negative views. The following points will help draw out and utilize negative viewpoints.

1. Encourage the person who expresses the negative viewpoint to talk. Find out just exactly what specific things are causing his negative attitude.

2. Express understanding and summarize his statement to the group as a sub-problem to be resolved by the group. Do not present the negative statement as something for the group to decide the importance of, rather, present it as an important element that needs to be resolved. The solution to the sub-problem may simplify the main problem.

3. Confront personal attacks. The purpose of the meeting is to develop ideas, not evaluate people. If someone attacks another person, ask what he is trying to accomplish or how his remarks relate to the problem. If this doesn't stop the verbal attacks, indicate that the personal arguments are making it difficult to solve the problem and that future remarks should be restricted to the problem.

4. State the solution recommended to overcome the cause of the negative view in a positive way. If the solution is expressed positively, the problem will escape the original connotation of negativism.

3. PROVIDING A SUPPORTIVE CLIMATE

Often people in meetings stop participating because they feel no one listens or really understands what they are trying to say. You can overcome this problem by using a technique originated by Dr. Carl Rogers (1957) that verifies listening and understanding.

One person is asked to express his views and a second person must summarize those views prior to presenting his own ideas. The process is continued with each new speaker first summarizing the views or ideas of the previous speaker.

As each person sees that he is understood, which usually requires a question or two with answers, he tends to relax and become more attentive to others and less stereotyped in his own thinking. The frustration that usually builds up due to lack of understanding or from competition for the right to speak is eliminated.

You can support each person's attempts at gaining understanding by showing each one that you understand him, even if no one else does. You can summarize his statements and indicate that you understand his feelings. Show that you see the problem from his viewpoint. He will then feel comfortable knowing that someone understands.

4. WORKING WITH A DEVIL'S ADVOCATE

A Devil's advocate is used to challenge the majority opinion. Often, in group meetings, the members unconsciously form a non-competitive alliance. In trying not to be competitive, they stop challenging each other. When one member of the group makes a suggestion, everyone automatically agrees with that suggestion. When this happens the opportunity for innovative or creative solutions is lost.

The most productive problem-solving groups are those that bring the entire range of knowledge possessed by the group to bear on the problem. This knowledge normally comes out during discussion. By comparing and contrasting ideas, by questioning, challenging and pointing out weaknesses or previously unseen problems, the knowledge of the group is drawn out.

When the group members are not questioning or challenging each other, you should appoint a Devil's advocate. His job is not limited to looking for weakness in a proposition. He should make sure that the advantages and disadvantages of a proposal are both discussed. This permits the advantages to be retained and the disadvantages to be explored for correction.

A Marketing Meeting That Was Guided by a Devil's Advocate. Carl, the branch manager of a manufacturing plant, called his product and marketing managers together to discuss the decline of one of their major product lines. The marketing manager for the product in question was asked to give his ideas first.

Fred, the product marketing manager, very optimistically stated, "We are going to increase our sales substantially next quarter. I've put the word out to the salesmen that we must have immediate action." Bill, the sales manager, played the role of the Devil's advocate. Bill asked, "Fred, are you aware that the entire industry is trending downward and that demand for your product has been greatly reduced?"

Fred, in an overly optimistic voice said, "We are going to increase our sales in spite of the downtrend." Bill asked, "How?" Fred replied, "We'll push harder than our competition." Bill continued questioning Fred about the techniques he would use, how he would encourage dealer participation and what would happen if the consumer would not purchase additional product.

Fred began to see he needed more than enthusiasm to do the job. Due to this prodding from the Devil's advocate, Fred realized that he would have to commit substantial funds for advertising and promotion, if he were to have any chance of success. When all the possibilities were examined, it became clear that Fred's sights would have to be lowered to a more realistic level. A promotional budget was developed in line with the lowered expectations.

OVERCOMING BARRIERS TO GROUP SOLUTIONS

The barriers that hinder solutions in group meetings are generally psychological. The two main psychological barriers are "hidden issues" which are held by group members and the "undue influence" of a superior. The "hidden issues" are related to fears that a group solution of one problem may result in a later action that will interfere with some project that a member wants no interference in. The "undue influence" of a superior results when group members fear reprisals if they disagree with the superior.

How to Avoid Undue Influence by a Superior

Try to keep the conversation going between group members rather than with the superior. If the other members keep talking, he may not feel it necessary to interject his view. When a superior does interject his opinions, you might lead the group back into discussion. You could do this by saying to the superior, "Is that what you want done or did you mean for us to discuss the problem further?" If he replies that further discussion is needed, you can then lead the group into further discussion. If you are the superior, withhold your own suggestions and ideas until everyone else has expressed his opinion. You will be much more likely to get opinions from others if you hold your own until they have an opportunity to discuss the problem without the pressure of having to disagree with the boss.

How to Surface and Neutralize Hidden Issues

If you feel that certain group members are opposing a point of view for reasons other than those being given, you can surface and neutralize those hidden issues. One way to do this is to ask the opposing person to describe his preferred solution. By examining the preferred outcome, you will find elements that you can compare and contrast with elements of the problem. This analysis may reveal the hidden issue.

Self-disclosure is another technique for getting other people to reveal their hidden issues. If you admit some concern or fear about the causes or possible outcomes of the solution, you may evoke the same disclosure from others. Your display of trust will often evoke the trust that permits disclosure of the hidden issues.

A third technique for evoking disclosure of a hidden issue is to suggest that there is some other reason for the opposition. People generally will reveal their true reasons rather than have false ones ascribed to them. This is especially true when it is clear that you can be trusted to hold the information confidential.

How Hidden Issues Were Surfaced in a Business Meeting. The vice president of marketing for a midwestern paper products distributor called a meeting between the managers of two distribution centers in a local midwestern city. One center distributed paper products to restaurants and the other center distributed similar products to retail food outlets.

The vice president proposed that the two distribution centers be combined into one in order to reduce expenses and streamline operations. Both local managers objected to the change.

The restaurant division manager objected that the change would make it impossible for him to properly service the restaurant trade. He explained the special service requirements that had to be met when dealing with restaurants. He concluded that a reduction in service would seriously affect his business.

The retail manager also resisted the change. He opposed the change because he believed the special handling of the many small orders required by restaurants would increase the overall cost of operations. He felt these additional costs would unfairly burden the retail accounts and eventually result in a drop in sales.

The vice president sensed that hidden issues were involved in each manager's resistance. In order to get information to work with, he asked both men to separately write up their recommendations for moving into one distribution center. The vice president said there would be substantial savings if the two men could find a way to make the change work. He concluded the meeting and asked that the written recommendations be completed within two weeks.

Both letters were in the vice president's office within the week. There were two elements in common: both managers recommended that the new center be divided and that they each report separately, directly to the vice president as they had in the past.

The vice president suspected and later verified that the hidden issue was one of autonomy. Both managers had been afraid of losing their authority in the new center. Both expected some new manager to be brought in and placed over both of them.

The vice president made the change, leaving each manager with his original authority. He asked them to work out the details of the move into the new center. Satisfied that they were each retaining their individual authority, they worked out an integrated system that substantially reduced costs for both divisions.

14

How to Predict What People Will Say and Do

People develop habitual responses to certain situations and these situations can be used as a guide in predicting individual behavior. When criticized, for example, most people become either defensive or argumentative. A few people respond appreciatively and ask for further details or advice on how they can improve. A few others withdraw and make no comment at all. What people say is determined by their internal needs. The way they say it, however, is affected by the external situation and by their perception of how people will react to what they say.

In this chapter, I will reveal techniques for predicting people's behavior. First, you'll learn to recognize the different personality traits that emerge in response to various internal psychological needs. Then, you'll see how to analyze these traits in relation to various situational changes and predict an individual's behavior under various conditions.

You'll see how a person changes his behavior to conform to his perception of his own power and the power of others. You'll see how to predict his behavior based upon these power relationships. By predicting what others are going to say, you can plan the things you need to say. This ability to predict and plan will give you the Psychological Leverage needed to double your effectiveness in all situations. If you practice these techniques, your effectiveness will increase rapidly.

PSYCHOLOGICAL PREDICTORS: FOUR MOTIVATIONS THAT INFLUENCE WHAT PEOPLE SAY

An individual develops consistent patterns of behavior in an attempt to keep his personality in balance. If he perceives himself as a kind humanitarian, he will consistently be kind and generous in his dealings with others. If he did not act in this way, he would have to admit to himself that he was not behaving in a manner consistent with his beliefs. He would then either develop guilt feelings or begin to change his perception of himself.

People may intensify or alter their behavior patterns when threatened or faced with situations beyond their ability to control. A person changes his behavior as a defense against a threat or uncontrollable situation. The defensive behavior may be an act of aggression, denial, repression, overcompensation, rationalization, projection, vacillation.

These altered behavior patterns also become habitual in response to certain situations. You might conduct certain tests to analyze a person's behavior over a period of time and determine his usual response to various situations. For example, you might make an obviously incorrect remark. The person's response of anger, silence, agreement or questioning will give you the insight into his personality.

There are four basic needs that motivate people. These needs are expressed in speech and are guidelines to what people will say in various situations. They are the needs for security, approval, recognition and self-actualization.

Verbal Reflections of Insecurity

According to Dr. A. H. Maslow (1954), security is man's second most important need. Man first directs his attention to the fulfillment of his biological needs, but once they are substantially satisfied, he becomes concerned with the need to feel secure. Security, on Maslow's scale or hierarchy of human needs, is the second most powerful determinant of behavior.

The loss or reduction of mental, physical or financial security causes man to feel tense or nervous. These feelings of insecurity motivate people's behavior. This internal tension motivates people to do or say something to restore their feeling of security.

Some people never feel secure. They always feel they are walking a tightrope that might give way at any time. These people have trouble taking actions that involve any risk. They tend to be overly conservative, avoid pressure, back away from problems and blame their failures or misfortune on someone else.

You can predict what these people will say in future conversations by analyzing their current and past remarks. A person who has blamed his wife for past financial failures will probably blame her again in the future. If he blames his boss for his job problems, his subordinates for his lack of organization or his customers for his lack of sales progress, you can expect him to continue this behavior in the future.

You can predict that this person will find someone to blame in every situation. When questioned about job goals and progress you can expect him to withhold information. He will generally try to qualify his answers with "maybe," "if I can," "I guess," "I'll try," or "I'll do whatever you say." He answers this way to avoid risk.

You can be prepared to deal with this type of person by thinking out the questions that will be asked in advance of any meeting with him. By thinking over his past behavior, you can determine who he will blame or what excuse he will make. You now have the psychological advantage of knowing in advance what he is going to say. You can use this knowledge to prepare your own remarks and questions to your own best advantage.

Verbal Predictors of Approval Needs

Just as some people are overly concerned about their security, other people may be even more concerned about approval. Maslow says the social needs, which include the need for approval, will motivate what they say and how they say it. A person who wishes approval for his social friendliness will probably be very agreeable with everyone who speaks.

People who seek approval from others tend to be very friendly, agreeable and willing to be taken advantage of in small matters. They generally do not see that they are being taken advantage of, however. They tend to make excuses for others and feel that accepting the disadvantage is actually a friendly act.

In conversation their motivation for approval tends to cause them to be overly agreeable. They'll say, "you are right," "I agree with you," "yes," "I know you must have thought it out," or "I believe everything you say." This person believes that approval comes only from constant agreement with others.

Once you have determined, through listening and observing, that a particular individual falls in this category, you can predict what he will say in future conversations. He will say nice sweet things only and will agree with everything whether he believes it or not.

"Recognition Blindness"

Closely related to the need for approval is the need for recognition. The behavior exhibited by people who overemphasize the need for recognition is quite different from the submissive behavior exhibited by the person seeking approval. The person who is overly concerned with the need for recognition may be described as having "recognition blindness." He is so intent upon making his knowledge and skill known to others that he is blind to his own behavior.

This person may be a braggart. He may continually talk about the great things he has done. At every opportunity he will talk about his accomplishments. If you tell a story of some success you had, he will tell a bigger one. His speech will be characterized by "I," "I can," and "I am."

You can predict his future behavior in any situation. He will always try to tell others how things should be done. He will be the first to tell others they are wrong, but will argue to the end to protect his own opinions. You can study this type of individual and be prepared. Knowing what he is most likely to say will help you prepare what you wish to say. Perhaps you can help remove his blinders.

The Need for Self-Realization

Aristotle said, "The goal of all human activity is self-realization." Maslow found that self-actualization, the highest level of his hierarchy of needs, is an on-going need that is never completely realized. As man reaches his potential in one area of endeavor, he finds new interests and new challenges. Although he may completely satisfy his needs for security, approval and esteem, he will never completely satisfy his need for self-realization.

The person who is motivated by the need for self-realization is a person seeking additional knowledge and information. He looks for challenges that will lead to improvement and help him reach his potential. He asks questions, he looks for facts and figures, he wants evidence, he asks for opinions and he carefully evaluates what you say.

You may not be able to predict what this person will say, but you can predict his approach or the way he will say it. You can be sure he will ask questions and more questions. He'll ask for comparisons with other systems. He'll want to know the advantages and the disadvantages of each program you suggest. He'll want to know the most probable consequences of any action you recommend and he'll want to know what other alternatives are available for the same project.

An Operations Manager's Bid for New Machinery. Paul Blanchard, the operations manager of an eastern electronics firm, needed new equipment in order to improve productivity. One stamping machine was so old that production from the machine was down twenty per cent from the previous year. Paul asked for an appointment with his boss to discuss purchasing new machinery. George, Paul's boss, agreed, but advised Paul that it was difficult to get any expenditures through the new purchasing agent.

Paul knew the real problem was his boss. In the past George had always put things off, was afraid to do anything on his own and tried to avoid risk at all cost. Paul thought about what George would be likely to say. He predicted George would blame the new purchasing agent and say their profits were too low to warrant purchasing the new machine.

Paul went into his boss's office prepared. When, as predicted, George blamed the purchasing agent, Paul gave George a written request for the purchasing agent to evaluate a new machine's effect on productivity. George saw there was no risk for himself, so he agreed.

When the purchasing agent came to investigate the old machine, Paul had prepared waste figures for all the machines on the floor as well as waste projections for the new machinery. The purchasing agent recommended immediate replacement of two machines and suggested a schedule for replacing all the old equipment in the plant.

THREE SITUATIONAL VARIABLES THAT INFLUENCE THE WAY WE SPEAK

Our motivation to take action is internally generated. Our desire to speak or act results from those internal tensions that develop due to our physical and mental needs. The way we carry out those actions however, is determined by our perception of what the consequences of our actions will be.

If we believe that "the squeaking wheel gets the grease," we may interpret that to mean that we can get more by complaining, by shouting or simply by quietly bringing attention to our needs. Our individual perceptions differ and consequently each of us acts differently.

We also act differently depending upon our perception of the situation. If we perceive ourself as the strongest member of a group, we may tend to be more dominant in that group. If we see ourself as the weakest member, we will behave more submissively. There are three basic situational variables that may affect our perception of consequences and alter our behavior. The three variables are:

1. The Situational Power Factor
2. The Speaker's Behavioral Habits
3. The "Personality-Interaction" Variable

The Situational Power Factor

When one person has organizational power that is higher than any other person there, his behavior will reflect his personal needs. He may assume a somewhat more dominant stance than usual, because he is the most powerful person there. You need only look at the psychological predictors to determine what he is likely to say.

When you have the highest organizational power, you may expect others to take a somewhat submissive role. Regardless of the fact that they seem dominant in other situations, they will tend to be submissive when talking to you. The insecure person will become even more insecure, the person seeking approval will place emphasis on agreeing with your every word. Even the guy with the "recognition blinders" on will alter his behavior. He will still seek recognition by relating his "I am" stories, but he will not challenge you. He will accept your ideas and opinions. He may reject them later, but he will not openly do so.

You can predict his behavior based on his past association with you. You can utilize the knowledge of what he will say to win his support. Just letting him feed his ego a little will cause him to respond favorably to you.

The person who is motivated by self-realization needs will generally not act differently when confronted with different power situations. He is motivated to learn and grow and he will try to do that in all situations. His previous behavior in one situation may be generalized and extrapolated to new situations.

The Speaker's Behavioral Habits

The person who has developed the habit of criticizing people in everyday situations may be expected to do the same in a meeting. If you have seen someone constantly criticizing his fellow employees or friends, you may expect him to do the same in a new situation.

A person who is aggressive with his friends will be aggressive when placed in charge of other people. If a salesman is promoted to sales supervisor and is antagonistic to the salesmen, he has probably been antagonistic to others in the past.

By watching the everyday habits of people you can predict their future actions. A person who uses profanity can be expected to continue to do so. A person who continually interrupts others can be expected to continue to do so. You can listen, observe and predict what they will say in other situations.

The "Personality-Interaction" Variable

Interactions between people are always complex and the difference in personalities have an impact on the behavior of all parties involved in an interaction. A person who is normally aggressive may, when reacting to certain personality types, become submissive. In other situations he may become more aggressive. A person whom you have categorized as withdrawn and submissive may suddenly become hostile and aggressive.

Then sudden behavior changes at first glance may seem to destroy your model for predicting what others will say. On closer examination, you will find that they actually provide a more reliable base from which to predict what people will do and say in various situations. The following examination of interactions between people of differing motivations will illustrate this point.

If two people who are both strongly motivated for recognition engage in conversation they will most likely become argumentative. As soon as one of them expresses an opinion that is contrary to an opinion held by the other, an argument will begin. Each, with his "recognition blinders" on, will be so interested in achieving recognition for himself that he will verbally attack the other.

When you know that two people who are both overly concerned with recognition are going to be involved in a meeting, you can

predict some antogonistic behavior with a high probability of success. If one of the two has more power in the organization, the
behavior will most likely be different. The one with less power will
restrain himself.

If there is another person in the meeting who is motivated by
feelings of insecurity, his submissiveness will be the same as usual
but his submissiveness may evoke hostility from the more dominant
members. This would only occur when the submissive person becomes involved in direct discussion with a more dominant member.

Psychologists have found that submissiveness, in a personal
interaction with a dominant person, evokes hostility from the more
dominant person. The more dominant a person is, the more he is
irritated by submissive people. Dominant people seem to feel dis-
gusted when other people won't stand up for their rights.

Sometimes submissive people become very aggressive and lash
out against those who provoke them. This occurs as a result of more
pressure than usual, or as the final straw falls when a number of other
pressures have been building up. Everyone has a limit to his tolerance; when this limit is surpassed, he "blows up." An accumulation
of nonrelated pressures or a single longstanding pressure can significantly lower this tolerance level. Then the usually restrained
person "blows" at the slightest provocation. The following checklist
will help you predict when a person will "blow" and what he will say:

1. Analyze each person's past behavior to determine his motivations.
2. Evaluate the situational variables to determine the power of
   each person.
3. Analyze each person's motivations to determine the position
   each is likely to take on the issue in question.
4. Base your prediction on what each person will say on your
   analysis of steps one through three.
5. Prepare your own remarks to capitalize on what you expect
   the others to say.

**How an Operations Manager Used Psychological Predictors to
Change the Outcome of a Meeting.** Paul Blanchard, operations manager for an electronics firm, received a note from George Mitner, the
plant manager. The note requested Paul and his production foreman,
Bill Evans, to attend a meeting the following Friday to discuss the
plant's production problems.

During the last eighteen months, Bill had increased production
by twenty per cent, but his employee turnover rate had increased to

twenty five per cent per year. Now that a large number of the employees were new, production was starting to decrease. Last month, production was down two per cent and the daily figures were beginning to look as if there would be a larger decrease in the current month.

Paul began to think about the past behavior of Bill, the production foreman, and his boss George. Paul recognized that the biggest part of the problem was caused by Bill's behavior. In the past Bill had been very pushy. He made unreasonable demands on the workers and constantly "rode" them to improve their production. Bill made no allowance for the different levels of skill the men had. He pushed them all for the maximum their machines were capable of producing. The new men had very little training and Paul believed they were actually doing worse than they were capable of because of Bill's unreasonable demands. Paul thought that Bill was motivated to win recognition as a top flight, tough managing foreman.

Paul also thought about George. George was fearful and always finding someone to blame. He was easily talked down and seemed to be motivated by security needs. Even though George had more organizational power, Paul believed that unless he personally interfered, Bill would assume the position of power in the meeting. Paul decided to exert leadership in the meeting and assume the power himself in order to direct the discussion to the real problem.

Analyzing the individual motivations and the situational variables, Paul predicted that Bill would blame the worthless employees he was saddled with and recommend tighter supervision, more control and tougher treatment. George, he believed, would jump at the chance to find someone to blame and accept Bill's reasoning. Paul decided to prepare a plan to correct the errors that would zero in on the real problem. The problem as Paul saw it was the lack of training for the new employees and the unreasonable demands made upon them.

Paul's predictions were accurate. At the meeting, Bill immediately began to complain about the new worthless employees. Paul agreed that the new employees were the problem. He stopped Bill at that point, however, and said he had developed a plan to train the new employees.

Paul's new plan required that new employees be given six weeks of basic instruction, during which time there was to be no quota. They would be given quotas starting with the seventh week and the quotas would be gradually increased on a weekly basis until maximum efficiency was achieved. No individual criticism was to be employed so that morale could be improved. The total daily production figures would be given to the group so they could evaluate their own progress.

Paul's analysis of what George and Bill were likely to say helped him prepare for the meeting. He was able to plan a strategy based on his predictions. He was successful in getting the plan adopted because it was directed at correcting the new employees' lack of proficiency. Since Bill had blamed the new employees, he was obligated to support a plan for correcting the problem.

15

How to Use Psychological Leverage as a Key to Personal Success

'

In this concluding chapter I will show how to use the techniques you have learned in this book to insure your personal success. You'll learn how to further your career goals by using speech techniques and your natural problem-solving ability. You can talk like, act like and be an expert in your field. By developing an image as an expert, you will move rapidly ahead in your chosen career.

The techniques covered in this chapter will help you improve your effectiveness in all areas of your life. A few simple steps will insure that you get better results, that you find more and better solutions to your problems and consequently establish a reputation as one of the outstanding people in the organization or group you belong to. This reputation will help you push ahead and more rapidly achieve your goals.

THREE WAYS TO DEVELOP A FAVORABLE IMAGE

One way to insure your success is to develop a favorable image. If you want to be looked at as a person worthy of promotion, people must hold a favorable image of you. If you wish to become a leader or have influence on other people, again, people must hold an image of you as a qualified leader or a person who has a great amount of knowledge in a particular field. There are three simple ways to develop the favorable image you desire. They are the development of an image as an expert, the use of speech techniques that leave a positive impression and the selection of words that enhance results

1. HOW TO ESTABLISH AN IMAGE AS AN EXPERT

There are three main characteristics that denote expertise in any field. These characteristics remain the same for all experts, regardless of the level of expertise. Research has shown that people who have been classified as experts or who have been considered experts by their peers have differed widely in the actual amount of knowledge they held about their area of expertise. One study found that, of a group considered to be experts in economics, nearly one-third of the group had only a very basic understanding of the subject. Three characteristics shared by all members of the group of so-called experts were:

1. The member had written an article for a magazine or had made one or more speeches at a public gathering.
2. The member had developed a new innovation, product or system or had simplified the design of some operation.
3. The member behaved and spoke in a restrained and quiet manner. He listened more than he spoke, which was interpreted as a sign of intellectual reflection.

Developing Public Recognition

You can establish your own image as an expert by developing the three characteristics in your own area of interest. First of all, you probably know enough about your own profession, hobby, or some specialized interest to write the magazine article now. You need only to sharpen or develop your writing skills and then write the article. You can find a good book on writing at your local library or book store. If you feel you need more knowledge about writing, take an evening course at a local community college.

Before you commence writing, check the trade magazines of your industry to find out the kinds of articles they print. It will be much easier to get your article published, if you write one similar to those appearing in the magazine you choose. No publisher is going to change the format of his magazine to fit your article. Your article will have to fit their format or it simply won't be used.

If you choose the speech route rather than the writing route, you can progress very rapidly to develop speaking ability by joining some club such as the Toastmasters. The Toastmasters Club is dedicated to helping its members improve their speaking and leadership skills. There are commercial and college courses available also, if you do not wish to join a club.

Developing the "Company Innovator" Reputation

The second characteristic of an expert, developing a new innovation, may at first seem very difficult or impossible. If you look
closely, however, you will find ample opportunity for improvement.
Look for the non-productive expenditures that exist in every company. If you can find areas where time and money are being expended
without a return that justifies the expenditure, you will be able to
establish yourself as an expert by developing a proposal that reduces
these expenditures to a reasonable level.

Every organization has enough overlap between various departments that you should be able to develop new systems that will
eliminate the duplication of expenses. Consultants have found so
much waste in the average organization that they can guarantee to
find at least ten percent waste in any department they investigate.

So, look for the high expenditure areas in your department.
Once you have found an area of high expenditure, isolate the time
segments and the money segments and then analyze the system and
see what time and money segments can be eliminated. If a first
analysis doesn't expose any areas of excess expenditures of time or
money, then set a goal for a ten percent reduction of expenses. If the
situation is one where there are no logical ways to reduce time or
money expenditures, then set the goal as an improvement of ten
percent without regard for how the improvement will be effected.

When you have established the goal, you can then begin looking
for solutions. Make lists of possible changes that will give you the
results you are trying to achieve. You may rearrange the work layout,
simplify the current design, design a completely new system, develop
a use for some by-product, find new uses for your current product or
find some new innovation that will simplify production. Once you
list all the possibilities and think about them every day, your natural
problem-solving ability will help you find the answer.

Developing the "Quiet Intellectual" Characteristic

The third way to establish an image as an expert is to speak in a
quiet and restrained manner. This doesn't mean to speak in a low
monotone voice so that people are unable to hear or understand you. It
means not to become loud and obnoxious. Speak firmly and convincingly with proper inflections, raise your voice to make points or to
make sure people hear you, alter your voice level from higher to lower
volume but always speak politely and with restraint. You can't force

your ideas on other people and you can't make them accept your logic by raising your voice. You can gain their understanding by calmly and rationally expressing your point of view   .

How a Favorable Image Helped a Product Manager's Career. A friend of mine was a product manager, early in his career, for a West Coast beverage company. A product manager at that time was a combination marketing, sales and production coordinator. He was more a generalist than a specialist, as the usual promotional route to product management was through the sales division.

He told of one vacancy, however, that was filled by a product manager that came up through production. He was transferred in from an out-of-state plant that had no sales force. The usual procedure in the other plant was to promote product managers from their production department. So the new product manager was a specialist and an expert in his field.

The new product manager knew the value of having an image of an expert. Upon arrival, he immediately established himself as an expert by making a thorough inspection of all facets of the production process. He checked incoming raw material and established new methods for quality control inspections. He checked production methods and made suggestions that reduced waste. He checked bottling and warehousing and made recommendations for better inventory control. Everyone was shown that he was an expert.

In a few months he was promoted to a product group supervisor. Now he was responsible for the supervision of three product managers. The first thing he did, as group supervisor, was sign up for night school. He took a public speaking course so that he could better get his ideas across to his subordinates. He was so successful that a year later he was promoted to sales manager.

When he became sales manager, he immediately began to look for new ways to increase sales. He looked for new innovations in products, for new techniques in selling and new ways to get more customers. He found new customers, developed new promotional programs and suggested new products and changes in old products to better fill his customers needs. Again, he was successful.

Two years later, he was promoted to Branch Manager. He did an excellent job as Branch Manager. One reason that he was promoted to and was successful as a branch manager was his quiet and restrained manner. His quiet speech coupled with his persistence and inner determination to succeed helped him establish the image that led to his success as a manager.

2. HOW TO USE SPEECH TECHNIQUES TO ESTABLISH A POSITIVE IMPRESSION

There are five major techniques that you can use to be sure that you make a good impression on the people you deal with. By carefully following this five-step guideline in all your interactions with people, you will develop the Psychological Leverage of having people place more weight on what you say. You can develop this ability to make a positive impression by showing courtesy, developing confidence, displaying poise, acting friendly and improving your diction.

Showing Courtesy

You can show courtesy by listening to and reflecting on the comments that other people make. If you carefully analyze what other people say and respond to their comments you are showing that you feel they are important enough to deserve your courtesy. It is courteous to listen quietly, without interrupting, until the other person has completely finished talking. If you are not sure when he has finished, ask him if he is through. While you are listening and thinking, the other person will see you as a person who thinks intellectually about other people's problems. Listening, then, helps you establish an image as a quiet intellectual at the same time that you are showing courtesy.

You can also show courtesy in the way that you respond to the opinions and problems of the other person. By showing that you empathize with the problems of the other person, you help him think clearly and develop confidence that he can solve his own problems. It would also be courteous to offer to help him solve the problem, if you have any way to help.

Developing Confidence

Confidence builds upon itself. To develop confidence be aware of your posture, hold your head up, speak clearly, project your voice and speak with conviction. Show that you have no doubt about anything you say. If you are engaged in a discussion about something that you are not sure about, then speak just as convincingly about your doubts. If you speak with confidence and act confident you will develop the confidence you need to show others that you are confident.

You can show your confidence by being enthusiastic, but don't become so enthusiastic that you say things that you are unsure of or that aren't true. If you use unreliable evidence or information that is not valid, you will lose your own reliability. Over time, people will learn that they can't rely on what you say. So, you will have the reputation of an enthusiastic liar, rather than a confident person.

You can also show your confidence by showing self-control. A person who has confidence in his ability to handle all situations will have no need to lose his temper. If something happens that makes you feel angry, don't show the anger. You can slip away quietly and "blow your top" out of sight of your audience. You can also imagine or picture yourself "blowing your top" to help relieve the tension of anger. The long-range solution, however, is to learn not to get angry. It is much more sensible and healthy, if you don't get angry at all.

In order not to get angry, you must develop the conscious desire to remain calm in all circumstances. The following techniques will help you remain calm and give you self-control:

1. Work off each day's hostility by growling, condemning or complaining in as loud a voice as is necessary while driving home or while taking your shower after you arrive home. This keeps you from being on edge due to a previous day's frustrations.

2. Make a list of the situations that make you angry, so you can be prepared for them. When they arise, tell yourself that you don't have to get angry to solve a problem or face a situation.

3. Write down exactly how you felt while you were angry. By learning to recognize the feelings that are associated with anger, you will recognize yourself becoming angry in time to take control of yourself.

4. Learn to look at anger-provoking situations as being incongruent with your personality. Then you can laugh at them. It is impossible to be angry while you are laughing.

5. Directly confront any situation that angers you, but do it in a non-aggressive way. If you settle each problem as it arises, you will not have a buildup of irritations that will cause you to be on edge all the time.

6. If you find you can't hold in your anger, then tell the other person that he is making you angry. Don't attack him, calmly point out the things that are making you mad.

7. Keep reminding yourself that anger is a hostile act, that argument never solved anything and that it is more healthy to laugh than to get mad.

One man, more than any other, displayed continual confidence during World War II. Whether fighting in Africa or France, he was always confident of his troops and himself. During the Battle of the Bulge a giant traffic tie-up was created among the military trucks, jeeps and tanks all trying to move through a muddy crossroad.

General Patton, the ever-confident commander, moved into the center of the tie-up and began personally directing the traffic. Whether due to the General's skill or presence, the traffic was soon moving in an orderly fashion. The General then walked back to his jeep confident that traffic would keep moving.

Displaying Poise

Displaying poise is displaying physical and mental balance. Many people who stand comfortably erect, well balanced, lose their mental poise by talking when they really have nothing to say. To be balanced in conversation is to refrain from speaking when you really have nothing to say. To be poised is to be comfortable with silence. Real poise evolves with confidence. When you feel confident of yourself in any situation, your poise will show. You will be relaxed and speak freely and spontaneously.

The knowledge of your strengths and weaknesses will help you develop poise. When a topic comes up that falls in an area of knowledge that you are strong in, you can confidently express yourself in that area. If you are truly poised, you can also handle those areas that you are weak in. By openly saying that you are not knowledgeable in the area being discussed, you retain your poise and establish an atmosphere that permits you to ask questions so that you may learn from the other people who are discussing the topic.

A Salesman Who Retained His Poise Under Adverse Conditions. A sales manager told a story about one of his salesmen, who he said never lost his poise. He accompanied this salesman on a sales call, in which the salesman was making a major presentation to the buying committee of a large retail chain.

The salesman always used a plastic sample bag in which he kept a sample of the product he was presenting. He kept the sample out of sight until the proper moment. This created interest, as everyone wondered what he had in the bag.

The salesman was very talkative but well organized. He would use a well-developed sales speech to describe his product and when he felt he had properly stimulated the buyer's interest, he would dramatically open the bag and thrust out the product.

On the day the sales manager accompanied him, the salesman was to present a promotion that would introduce a newly designed, non-returnable plastic bottle. To prepare for the meeting, the salesman asked the shipping foreman to put a sample of the new bottle in the sample bag while he talked to the sales manager about his presentation.

The salesman rehearsed his sales pitch with the sales manager. He reviewed the main points of his presentation. He talked about the research that had gone into selecting the colors, the engineering that had resulted in a lower cost plastic that the consumer could throw away and the promotional discount that was developed to insure a successful sale. At that point in the actual presentation, he would open the sample bag and show the product. The sales manager approved of the salesman's plan, so they picked up the sample bag from the shipping foreman and went to the chain's buying office.

When they were called before the buying committee, the salesman went through his sales presentation, just as he had for the sales manager. He became enthusiastic as he talked and described the fine flavor, the convenience of the new bottle, the finest product available. He opened the sample bag and turned it upside down on the table. Every member of the buying committee leaned forward to see the new non-returnable bottle.

Out of the sample bag fell a sample in a can. The foreman had packaged the wrong product. The salesman retained his poise. "If you think our plastic bottle is good," he said, "you should try this aluminum can. This can is the finest on the market today." The committee laughed, the salesman and sales manager laughed and an appointment was made to present the new plastic bottle at a later date.

Acting Friendly

The quickest way to establish a positive impression is to be friendly. Everyone likes to see a warm smile and hear a friendly greeting. Many people think that friendliness is a sign of weakness. It is not. Real strength does not have to be displayed, friendliness does. Real strength is the quiet inner strength that is assertive without loudness or hostility. It shows without being called to attention. So smile, relax, be yourself and speak in warm and friendly tones.

Improving Your Diction

One of the easiest ways to leave a good impression is to improve your diction. Most people are impressed when they hear eloquent speech. If you think about the people who most impress you, many of them have developed eloquent habits of speech.

One characteristic that helps movie stars, statesmen, radio and television announcers and all public speakers is the eloquence with which they speak. If they are not pleasant to listen to, if they don't speak clearly and aren't easily understood, you lose interest and form a poor impression of them.

You can develop eloquence in your own speech by improving your diction. You can improve by listening carefully to public speakers. One source of speakers is available on the nightly news. You can listen carefully to a variety of speakers and then pick out one to emulate during your improvement period. Try to emulate the speaker's pronunciation, inflection and rate of speech. This will help you detect the differences between your own and the public speaker's skill.

At first you may not see the differences between your own and the announcer's way of forming words and pronouncing them, but if you listen carefully, you will begin to recognize the differences. You can more quickly detect the differences by using a tape recorder. Tape record both your own version and the announcer's voice for playback and comparison.

Overcoming Lazy Speaking Habits. As you begin your improvement program, there are four specific areas that you will need to concentrate on in order to improve your diction and speak more eloquently. First, concentrate on the way you form your words. Rather than drawing out your words, clip them off smartly. Don't stretch out a word in order to find time to think up your next thought. Drawing out your words gives the impression of laziness Clipping off the words appropriately leaves a good impression, an impression of conversation and enthusiasm.

Adding Interest and Concern to Your Speech. You can add interest and concern to your speech by developing good enunciation. Be precise in your pronunciation rather than speak in a slurred or slovenly manner. Again, slurred speech indicates laziness or the lack of interest in or concern for what you are saying. If you have no concern for what you say, or if people hold that impression, they have no reason to listen to you. Proper pronunciation indicates interest, pride and concern for what you are saying.

Pronunciation is probably the easiest of the four improvement areas to master. You can utilize the dictionary for self-correction and the help of a friend to correct you when you make errors that you are not aware of.

Developing Speech Rhythm. The development of a rhythmical rather than a broken word pattern is the third and more difficult area of improvement leading to more eloquent speech. You can improve the rhythm of your speech with patience and practice. Again, your tape recorder is necessary if you are to make any real progress. You can tape a few sentences, record them, play them back and listen.

Analyze the playback to see if your speech is smooth and rhythmic or broken or choppy. After noting the words or phrases that you are having a problem with, practice them a few times and then record them again. After repeating this a few times, play back the first recording and see how much you have improved.

Eliminating Harsh-Sounding Speech. The fourth way to speak more eloquently and leave a more favorable impression is to control the breath you expel with your words. Audible breathing accompanying your words gives your speech a harsh sound. You can develop a more eloquent sound by subduing your breath. Either hold your breath and release it softly between phrases or release it very slowly and quietly as you speak.

3. HOW TO USE WORDS TO ENHANCE YOUR RESULTS

Often people don't receive the credit they deserve, due to the use of words that don't adequately convey what they have accomplished. By carefully thinking about the results you have achieved, by comparing them to what others are doing or what had been done in the past, you will be able to use the appropriate words to describe your accomplishments. There are three techniques that you can use to place your results in the best possible light. These techniques are: use positive terms to describe your results, relate to the areas of progress and speak of the future.

Use Positive Terms

Often people who challenge you about your results will have a negative attitude. No matter how good your results may be, they will keep digging for something wrong or keep looking at the negative side of things. You can overcome this problem by responding to all their questions in positive terms.

Be inspirational in your comments as well as being positive. Use terms such as, "We're improving," or "We're making progress."

When asked about a reduction in output or lower sales, you can reply that you are doing better than competition. Compare your market share with that of competition to show that you are still doing well on a comparative basis.

If you are being unduly criticized during difficult times, respond with, "We're doing well under the current conditions, but I'm sure we'll be able to do better soon." Bring up a specific area that you are doing well in and dwell on that area. Try to find more positive areas than the negative ones that have been brought up so that you look good on balance.

During the entire conversation, be enthusiastic and show that you intend to do your best. People only become critical of those who are not willing to try; they usually will overlook lower-than-usual results if they see that you are sincere in wanting to improve. Say that you'll put your best effort into the task and then do so. Let your superior know that he can count on you. You can be positive about your current results and at the same time show that you are willing to cooperate to make the improvements that he may desire.

Concentrate on Areas of Progress

You can enhance your results in the eyes of others most easily by concentrating on specific areas of progress. To do this, prepare some comparisons to use whenever called upon for information or whenever questioned about your results.

Three standard measures of performance that you can use are comparisons to previous results, comparisons to the current year's goals and comparisons to what other people are doing. You can have these figures ready and then either say, "We're doing better than last year," "We're doing better than our goals" or "We're doing better than the other division."

You might also compare against other goals of your own. You could say, "We're ahead of schedule" or "We've gotten our costs in line with our projections." The important thing is to find something positive, the ones that make you look good, and be prepared to use them.

Psychologically, you simply need to produce more positive statements than the number of negative statements produced by the other person. The more you outweigh the negatives with positives the more will your results be enhanced.

Speak of the Future

When you need additional positive statements to overcome current negative statements, get the additional positive ones from the future. Look over your plans for the future and what you can reasonably expect to do and convert those future plans into positive statements.

You will then be able to counter negative statements by saying, "We've set plans in motion that will pay off next year." Or, you might use one of the following: "We're going to start a new system next month." "There's a good chance we'll get a government contract next month." "We're working on a big sale that we expect to go through in the near future." "Looking at our future orders, we expect to end the year with our budgeted profit objective accomplished."

I don't mean that you should make statements that aren't true. But if you look at booking plans and changes that are sure to occur, you will be able to honestly develop the positive statements that you need to give you the Psychological Leverage to overcome any negative statements that are thrown at you.

How One Manager Used Positive Statements to Enhance His Results. Bob Johnson, a distribution unit manager for a midwest manufacturer of frozen foods, had problems in every area of his business. His freezer space was too small and many items were being damaged or misplaced due to the overcrowded conditions. Two of Bob's salesmen had quit and were now working for competitors. To make matters worse, the economy in Bob's district had become depressed and sales had fallen for two months in a row.

In the past, Bob's supervisor had concentrated on Bob's inventory control problem. He constantly challenged Bob to find a solution to protect the product against damage and loss. Bob saw this as an almost impossible situation to remedy. But now that the supervisor was more concerned with sales volume, Bob was in agreement with the supervisor's desire to increase sales.

Bob was always optimistic and enthusiastic and he retained this attitude during the crisis. When the supervisor next called and complained about the drop in sales, Bob stated, "We're getting a large share of the business in this depressed area, but I know we have to get more." When the supervisor asked about the two men that had resigned, Bob said he would have them replaced in a few weeks. "In the meantime," he said, "everyone else is working extra to make up for their loss."

The supervisor pointed out that their sales were developing a downtrend. Bob replied, "We're going to make extra efforts to change the trend. By the end of the month we'll be in much better shape." The supervisor asked if Bob would cooperate in a sales push to overcome their problems. Bob assured him that he would cooperate in any way to regain his profitability.

The supervisor then said he had checked the plant records and found that Bob had not ordered any product into his distribution unit for two weeks. Bob thought for a minute and replied, "It's true, we haven't ordered anything for two weeks and our stock is very low. But we have solved the inventory problem. You can find the things you look for now and we don't have any damaged product." They both laughed.

*   *   *

This book has covered a wide range of psychological techniques that you can use in your daily interactions with people. These techniques will help you provide guidance to others, gain acceptance and understanding, and get your point of view accepted and acted upon. If you practice these techniques and tie into the psychology of the other person, you'll double the power of what you say.

SUGGESTED FURTHER READINGS

Abelson, Herbert I., Ph.D. Persuasion, *How Opinions and Attitudes Are Changed.* 2nd ed. New York: Springer Publishing Co. 1970.

Barron, Frank X. *Creativity and Psychological Health: Origins of Personal Vitality and Freedom.* New York: Van Nostrand, 1963.

Buzzotta, V. R., and R. E. Lefton, Ph.D. and Manuel Sherberg.*Effective Selling Through Psychology: Dimensional Sales and Sales Management Strategies.* New York: Wiley Interscience, 1972. Copyright (c) 1972 by Psychological Associates, Inc.

Cartwright, D. and Zander, A. (eds.).*Group Dynamics,* 2nd ed.; Evanston, Ill.: Row, Peterson & Co., 1960.

Cason, Hulsey. "Common Annoyances: A Psychological Study of Everyday Aversions and Irritations." *Psychological Monographs,* Vol. 40, #2, 1930, pp. 1-216.

Dickens, Milton. Speech. *Dynamic Communications.* New York: Harcourt Brace Jovanovich, Inc. 1954.

Dittes, J. E. and H. H. Kelley. Effects of Different Conditions of Acceptance Upon Conformity to Group Norms. *Journal of Abnormal and Social Psychology,* 1956. pp. 100-107.

Feinberg, Mortimer A., Ph.D.*Effective Psychology For Managers.* Englewood Cliffs, N.J.: Prentice-Hall, Inc., 1965.

Freud, Sigmund. *Psychopathology of Everyday Life.* Trans. A. A. Brill. New York: The New American Library, Inc., n.d.

Georgopoulas, Basil S., Gerald M. Mahoney and Nyle W. Jones Jr. "A Path-Goal Approach to Productivity." *Journal of Applied Psychology.* Vol. 41, 1957, pp. 345-353.

Ghiselli, Edwin E. "Differentiation of Individuals in Terms of Their Predictibility." *Journal of Applied Psychology.* Dec., 1956.

Ginott, Haim G. *Between Parent and Child.* New Solutions to Old Problems. New York: MacMillan Co., 1973.

Gordon, Thomas. *Parent Effectiveness Training.* New York: Peter H. Wyden, Inc., 1970.

Gordon, William J. Synectics: The Development of Creative Capacity. New York: Harper & Row Publishers, Inc., 1961.

Hare, A. Paul, R. F. Bales and E. F. Borgatta. (eds). Small Groups. New York: Alfred A. Knopf., 1955.

Hayakawa, S. I. Language in Thought and Action. New York: Harcourt Brace and World, Inc., 1949.

Holman, Peter A. "Validation of an Attitude Scale as a Device for Predicting Behavior." The Journal of Applied Psychology, Oct. 1956.

Hovland, C., I. Janis and H. Kelley. Communications and Persuasion. New Haven, Conn.: Yale University Press, 1961.

Howell, William S. and Donald K. Smith. Discussion. New York: The Mac-Millan Co., 1956.

Katz, Daniel, et. al. Productivity, Supervision and Morale Among Railroad Workers. Ann Arbor, Michigan: Survey Research Center: University of Michigan, 1951.

Korda, Michael. Power: How To Get It, How To Use It. New York: Ballantine Books, 1976.

Leavitt, Harold J. Managerial Psychology. Chicago: The University of Chicago Press, 1958.

Lefton, R. E., Ph.D., V. R. Buzzotta, Ph.D. and Mannie Sherberg, Dimensional Management Strategies, St. Louis, Copyright 1970 by Psychological Associates, Inc.

Lewin, Kurt. Resolving Social Conflict. (Edited by Gertrude Weiss Lewin). New York: Harper & Brothers Publishers, 1948.

Likert, Rensis. The Human Organization: Its Management and Value. New York: McGraw-Hill Book Co., 1967.

Maier, N. R. F. "The Quality of Group Decisions as Influenced by the Discussion Leaders." Human Relations, 1950. pp. 155-174.

Maltz, Maxwell. M. D., F.I.C.S. The Magic Power of Self-Image Psychology. Englewood Cliffs, N.J.: Prentice-Hall, Inc. Copyright (c) 1964 by Dr. Maxwell Maltz.

Maslow, Abraham H. Motivation and Personality. New York: Harper and Row, 1954.

Mayo, Elton. The Social Problems of an Industrial Civilization. Boston, Mass.: Graduate School of Business, Harvard University, 1945.

McClelland, D. et. al. The Achievement Motive. New York: Appleton-Century-Crofts, 1953.

Merton, Robert K. Social Theory and Social Structure. New York: Free Press, 1957.

Minnick, Wayne C. The Art of Persuasion. 2nd ed. Boston: Houghton Mifflin Co., 1968. Copyright (c) 1957, 1968 by Wayne C. Minnick.

Morgan, Clifford T. Introduction to Psychology. New York: McGraw-Hill Book Co., 1961.

Nirenberg, Jesse S., Ph.D. *Getting Through To People.* Englewood Cliffs, N.J.: Copyright (c) 1963 by Jesse S. Nirenberg, Ph.D.

Perls, Fredrick. M.D., Ph.D., Ralph F. Hefferline, Ph.D. and Paul Goodman, Ph.D. *Gestalt Therapy. Growth in the Human Personality.* New York: Dell Publishing Co., Inc., 1951.

Perry, Helen S. and Mary Ladd Garvel. eds. *The Collected Works of Harry Stack Sullivan, M.D.; The Interpersonal Theory of Psychiatry.* Vol. 1, New York: W. W. Norton, White Psychiatric Foundation, 1953.

Rogers, Carl R., Ph.D. *On Becoming A Person. A Therapist's View of Psychotherapy.* Boston: Houghton Mifflin Co. Copyright (c) 1961 by Carl R. Rogers.

Porter, Lyman W. and Edward E. Lawler. *Managerial Attitudes and Performance.* Homewood, Ill.: Irwin Dorsey, 1968.

Price, Steven S. *How To Speak With Power.* New York: McGraw-Hill, 1959.

Prince, George M. Creative Meetings Through Power Sharing. *Harvard Business Review,* July-August, 1972.

Rogers, Carl R. and Richard E. Farson. *Active Listening.* Chicago: University of Chicago, 1957. Copyright (c) 1957 by Industrial Relations Center, The University of Chicago. Quoted passages reprinted by permission of the publisher.

Scheflen, Albert E., M.C. *Body Language and Social Order. Communication as Behavioral Control.* Englewood Cliffs, N.J.: Prentice-Hall, Inc., 1972.

Schein, E. H. and W. G. Bennis. *Personal and Organizational Growth Through Group Meetings.* New York: John Wiley, 1965.

Shaw, Malcom E. Assertiveness Training For Managers. Madison Wisconsin: *Training and Development Journal,* Sept., 1976.

Shostrom, Everett L. *Man, The Manipulator.* Nashville, Tenn.: Abingdon Press., 1967.

Stroh, Thomas F. *Effective Psychology for Sales Managers.* New York: Parker Publishing Company, Inc., 1974.

Vroom, Victor H. *Work and Motivation.* New York: John Wiley and Sons, Inc., 1964.

Ziller, Robert C. "Four Techniques of Group Decision Making Under Uncertainity." *Journal of Applied Psychology.* Vol. 41, Dec., 1957.